ACCIDENTAL GARDENS

PRAISE FOR ACCIDENTAL GARDENS

With his clarity, directness and humour, Rob Carney writes like Richard Brautigan in an age of ecological collapse. This collection of flash essays and poems is a journey through the absurdity, tragedy and black comedy of late-stage capitalist and consumerist America, weaving between despair and hope like sixty million spawning salmon. It is also a map that points us towards how the damage might be repaired—a reminder to open our eyes and to pay attention.

—Nick Hunt,
Where the Wild Winds Are and Editor at *The Dark Mountain Project*

As long as I can remember, I have hated poetry. Then, Rob Carney presented his work at the AWP Writer's Conference in Seattle Washington. I found myself breathless and amazed, dreading the end of each piece, fearing it was the last. To my immense relief, I discovered that Rob's work climbs off the page and embeds itself inside of the reader with the same sublime clarity and intimacy that so effectively captured and held my attention that dark, cold night in the Pacific Northwest.'

—March Twisdale, *Prose, Poetry & Purpose* and *Focus On!*

There are a few writers who don't disappointment me, ever. Kim Stanley Robinson. J.G. Ballard. Sappho. Maybe that's a weird list? I don't know. Rob Carney is on that list too. Rob Carney cuts through literary bloat like an angry and very funny tusked animal. An ironic saber-tooth. A compassionate rhino, compassionate because it doesn't have time for b.s. and because, also, and I mentioned this, he's funny. Even when tragic and, let's face it, things are sorta tragic right now. But you know that. What you don't know is that Rob Carney's *Accidental Gardens* will give you an emotional and ethical vocabulary to live in, a way to be that is neither falsely hopeful nor fashionably despairing. It will give you, and this is the word for it: goodhumanimalism.

—Christopher Cokinos,
Professor of English, Arizona Institutes for Resilience

ACCIDENTAL GARDENS

ROB CARNEY

First published 2021

NATIONAL LIBRARY OF AUSTRALIA

A catalogue record for this book is available from the National Library of Australia

National Library of Australia and State Library of South Australia Legal Deposit
Carney, Rob (1968) – Author
Accidental Gardens
ISBN – 978-1-925856-29-3 (pbk)
ISBN – 978-1-925856-30-9 (ebk)

Cover Júlia Palazzo.
Typeset by Stormbird Press with Century Gothic and Kazimir.

Stormbird Press is an imprint of Wild Migration Limited

Stormbird Press

Stormbird Press
PO Box 73
Parndana
South Australia, 5220
Australia
Phone (61 8) 8121 5841
Email production@stormbirdpress.com
Web www.stormbirdpress.com

The publishing industry pulps millions of books every year when new titles fail to meet inflated sales projections—ploys designed to saturate the market, crowding out other books.

This unacceptable practice creates tragic levels of waste. Paper degrading in landfill releases methane—a greenhouse gas emission 23 times more potent than carbon dioxide.

Stormbird Press prints our books 'on demand', and from sustainable forestry sources, to conserve Earth's precious, finite resources.

We believe every printed book should find a home.

CONTENTS

May 6, 2020

DEAR AUSTRALIA,

I'm sorry. Those words aren't big enough, I know—not nearly—not in response to a continental firestorm. They'd need to be able to stretch and widen, like a river from Perth to Sydney. But I'm saying I'm sorry anyway because I am.

One of the places destroyed was the western end of Kangaroo Island, home to Stormbird Press. They lost their offices. The publishers, Geoff and Margi Prideaux, lost their house. And so many animals, so many trees, so much of so much. We'd planned for this book to be out today, but instead there's been devastation. Stack on a global pandemic, and the release date got delayed.

You and I are different—bits of lingo, the views out our windows, dingoes and kangaroos instead of pronghorn and coyotes—but I think that you'll get what I'm saying in these pages. And hopefully you'll laugh, maybe nod in agreement, maybe ask someone to sit for a second and listen while you read a bit out loud. I like those possibilities.

Six things I don't like, but I'll mention them just briefly:

Wayne LaPierre
Scott Pruitt
Ryan Zinke
Jeff Sessions
Betsy DeVos
and the DMV.

I name them in the book but know they might not be familiar. If that's the case, and if you want to know more, I'm tacking on a P.S. down below.

This isn't a book about political scum, though. I focus more on landscapes; on cherries and herons and salmon, and orcas and hawks and Australia, and stories and memory and rain because the best things deserve our attention more than the worst. Also, of course, because the best things need it.

That way we'll remember to protect them before they're gone.

Best wishes,
Rob Carney

PS: *The DMV* (Department of Motor Vehicles) is the place you go to get your driver's license. Ask anyone in America—it doesn't matter which town—and they'll tell you it sucks. *Scott*

Pruitt was a fossil fuels lobbyist, then the Head of the EPA (Environmental Protection Agency). Also, the guy was a weirdo. He had this soundproof cube installed in his office where he'd scuttle away to make his telephone calls. *Wayne LaPierre* of the NRA (National Rifle Association) is a lot like Tolkien's Gollum, but instead of a magic ring for his "precious," it's an endless clip of ammo. *Ryan Zinke* was Secretary of the Interior, and to prove it he liked to ride around on a horse. Then he'd hop down, open up a map, and draw an X through a National Park. *Betsy DeVos* was born into billions, so was her husband, and she hates public schools; she calls them "government schools." Trump appointed her to be his Secretary of Education. *Jeff Sessions* was Attorney General, but he seemed to think he was a Pharisee. In defense of federal actions along the U.S. southern border, he told reporters to read Romans 13—as in, the Bible—rather than the law. What actions on the southern border?—far too many, and they're all unjust. Type "child separations" in a search engine sometime, and you'll see.

INTRODUCTION TO ACCIDENTAL GARDENS

By Simmons B. Buntin

Yesterday I drove the two hours from my home in Tucson, Arizona, to the Whitewater Draw Wildlife Area, a collection of managed wetlands, trails, and viewing decks a few miles north of the Mexico border. Sandhill cranes by the tens of thousands overwinter here—their graceful necks and gray plumage, their red-capped heads and long black beaks, their raucous, rattling conversations overpowering any other noises except, perhaps, the occasional U.S. Customs and Border Protection Sikorsky helicopter.

Though I had come to experience the vastness of this high-desert landscape and the birds that call it their home, I also felt it important to ask them whether—as our President only days ago declared—there is a national emergency at the border. I had passed two Border Patrol checkpoints on the way down (pulling over only those heading north), as well as Tombstone, home to the most famous shootout in the Old West. I figured the cranes—who have been migrating across North America for at least 2.6 million years—have been around long enough to know an emergency when they see one. Most of their species' timeline, of course, was before the time of nations, but who's to suggest our President doesn't hold the collective wisdom of the eons?

I had planned this February visit between two seminal events: doing my taxes, which I had scheduled for the day after my session with the cranes, and reading Rob Carney's *Accidental Gardens*—this very book you hold now—which I had finished just a few hours before my road trip. My conversation with the Sandhill cranes on that brisk afternoon would serve as an appropriate bridge between the delightful conversation I had been having with Carney in the pages of this book and the conversation with the IRS (well, with the TurboTax bots) I was dreading. Call it my "Stopping by Woods on a Snowy Evening" transition—what I wanted to do versus what I had to do. That the President had opened another line of discourse between me and the cranes with his declaration was unexpected, but fitting.

My consultation with the cranes was, I admit, hit and miss. For one thing, they weren't keen to talk about the President's national emergency along the border when their wisdom spoke to a longer emergency spanning nations and the changing climate of the world. But they recognized that the President and his featherless buddies were already doing a lot of damage on public lands—a term a bit ridiculous to the birds, a species older than the hills surrounding Whitewater Draw. (I don't mean to imply the cranes were ill-mannered or had a short span of attention for my questions; rather, they weren't much concerned with the affairs of the day, beyond a slow grasshopper on a reed or the wind quickening out of the west.) Finally, just as I thought I was making headway, the cranes lifted en masse—the cerulean sky flush with the silhouettes of these long-winged vases in flight—and I was left in the shower of their riotous calls to answer for myself these other questions of the day.

Which is where Carney and this book come in (or rather, come in again). While the Sandhill cranes of Whitewater Draw weren't much for Q&A, here you'll find that the essays and poems of this collection are not just clever and poetic dialogue—though there is that. Rather, they are a conversation between the author and you, the reader. It's a conversation both whimsical and serious, with tight turns and lines enjambed, with seemingly disconnected elements coming together beautifully. From Halloween to humpback whales to Rainier cherries to Miles Davis—and that's just one essay.

"[A]n imagined town is just as real as an actual town," writes Richard Hugo in *The Triggering Town*. Carney's rich imagination is what seeds these conversations, and from the real challenges of the day—the preservation of public lands, supporting our education system, the salvation of craft in its many important contexts—he spins tales and wisdom from which any creature as far back as the Pliocene would take heart. (I'm looking at you, Sandhill cranes.) But you too, friend, are that surviving creature—and so are all of us under Carney's delightful, political, philosophical writing.

In a world of alternative truths, Carney gives us the real truth, one only possible through the mind and pen of a poet-essayist. Yet he insists, "I don't have a grand point I'm making here or anything. I'd rather just offer up one of my moon poems and hope it orbits in your thoughts awhile." And it's a lovely poem, but don't let the author's humility fool you—there is a grand point to the work in this collection, and that is this: Just as the stubbly fields and marshes of Whitewater Draw need the cacophony of crane calls, so we too need voices like Rob Carney's. Like the lead in that long skein of birds on the horizon, they direct us in troubling times and help us decipher emergencies real from emergencies imagined. They humor us, they center us, they free us. Prepare to take flight.

I.

ENVIRONMENTAL STUDIES

ARCHAEOLOGY

Who knew the badgers of Utah were so advanced? Not you. It's no use pretending you did. No, the only people who knew this were Mike Noel and me.

I'll tell you about my own credentials in a minute, but here are his: He's the state representative from Kanab; he's opposed to designating more national monuments; and back in June 2016, during interim meetings, he said something interesting. It had to do with the Bears Ears Monument, which is a longer story than I want to catch you up on, but the short version goes like this: Archaeologists by the hundreds sent a petition to President Obama—they wanted him to designate a Bears Ears monument in order to stop the looting of artifacts—and what

Representative Noel had to say about it was pretty great. He said, "There is no immediate threat. It's a scam. There's no fresh digging. All we can see today are badger holes. We have got to get a handle on these badgers because those little suckers are going down and digging up artifacts and sticking them in their holes."

Badger antiquities thieves! Oh man. And from the photo evidence ("F**k you BLM," carved in a rock; bullet holes in a petroglyph) these badgers are fluent in English and carrying guns.

Now, my own credentials aren't political. Me, I just collect odd details, then dust them off and display them the best that I can. My brother Colin, for instance, had some good ones after driving buses in Alaska. He came home awestruck that tourists could be so dumb. When I wondered what he meant by that, he told me some of the things they asked him. Then I went away with a pen and came back with a scrap of brotherly sympathy. I know it's no Grecian Urn, but it made him laugh:

IF YOU ASK A STUPID QUESTION IN ALASKA...

"Is this the same moon I see in Iowa?"
"No."
"Are these the same stars as Illinois?"
"Not quite. See, up here the Big Dipper's a saucepan to
simmer the Northern Lights, and the moon above Denali is
solid iron. We can pan the air for gold."
"Do polar bears eat people?"
"Not if they're full."
"Well, what about a moose?"
"Of course. Them too. Amazing hunters. Whenever tourists
vanish, it's a safe bet a well-fed moose is contentedly asleep."

"Are you pullin' my leg?"
"Do you want to see my scars?"
"So what's the elevation of Anchorage?"
"Probably four. It's right on the water."
"Ha ha, now I know you're lyin'. We're too far north... Hey, what do you call all these trees?"
"We call them the woods. Legends say the bark makes you smarter. Give one a lick."

This Utah badger detail reminds me of that. And it explains so many things succinctly. For instance, there's a high-rise going up where there used to be a toy store. It blocks—which hardly seems possible—our neighborhood view of the Wasatch Mountains. This is just the latest make-over/burial of a once unique area called Sugar House, and throughout this whole construction blitz there's been a moratorium on mitigation funds. Why? Good question, but I'm afraid there isn't a good answer. No, the money that builders normally pay for improvements to parks, road maintenance, increased fire and police protection to go along with thousands more cars and residents, and so on, is instead just money that the builders get to keep. It's been decades since I took Algebra, but the equation looks something like this: Call builders x and long-time residents and businesses y, where x = $$ and y = *@!?*! Yes, it's a lot to put up with, but it helps to know that our former mayor, Ralph Becker, made this decision while hypnotized by badgers.

What else? Badgers have pick-axed common sense and pirated it away. That's why doctors need insurance but gun owners don't. One is in case of malpractice; I get it. But shouldn't we call getting shot malpractice with a gun?

What else? You're a football fan, and the referees are terrible. Tell me their uniforms don't look a lot like badgers.

What else? Say you can't find joy. Or reason. Or an adequate, merited pay raise. Grab yourself a flashlight and crawl inside a badger hole. They're probably there beside some artifacts, clawed a bit but still valuable, brushed off and lined up on badger shelves. Take it from me and Mike Noel.

POLITICAL SCIENCE

One summer the people of Kalispell had too much paint. Driving into town, I saw a car slap-dashed with yellow—must have been two-hundred cartoon lemons—and a homemade signboard bolted on the roof: "Dale's Sales Auto / Lemon Car / No Good." So that was the first example.

The second was this: I was driving a truckload of fireworks to Sandpoint, Bonner's Ferry, Whitefish, etc.; Shelby, Great Falls, and Fort Benton, then back to Spokane, the same loop I'd taken three days before when I went to put up a dozen fireworks stands. So now I'm back in Kalispell, dropping off their order, and they've painted the whole stand with Jesus murals, wow—Son of God with a sparking halo; Messiah with a lamb in one hand, a Roman Candle in the other; one of the Wise Men, Melchior I think, putting Pop-Its in front of the manger—and the Youth Director running things had even more ideas:

"Why don't you sell some Christian fireworks? Instead of these Red Devils. You could add a sticker so people know they're Christian Approved."

"I don't pick the names," I told him. "They make them over in China."

He walked off talking about communists, shaking his head.

Our warehouse was happier, though, calling out test-run firework names, our typically boring and cardboard jobs suddenly not.

"How 'bout the *Star of Bethlehem*."

"And the *Noah Sees a Sunbeam*."

"Or the *30 Pieces of Silver*."

"Or *Let-There-Be-Lights*."

"Maybe the *Cleopatra*?"

"That's not biblical, you idiot."

"I thought she was married to Moses."

"What're you, nuts?"

"What should we call these *Piccolo Petes*?"

"*Little Towers of Babel*."

"How 'bout the *Cuckoo Fountains*?"

"Just call them *Doves*."

"Are you sure she didn't marry Moses? I thought I saw it in a movie."

"You think we should re-name the sparklers?"

"No, they're just sparklers. But now with myrrh!"

All of us channeling Byron or something, a bunch of low-wage Shakespeares stopping to sneeze black powder on our sleeves, and forgetting about our coffee break; that afternoon flew faster than any of us knew.

But why stop there? Why not specialize for everyone? Aim fireworks at nurses and doctors, cats and dogs. For the dinosaur lover, there's the *Pterodactyl Rocket.* For summer-league baseball teams we've got *Grand Slams.* For the ambidextrous, try these aerials with fuses on both sides. Everything lasered into segments, everything split. Even for surfers—two distinct versions of the *Perfect Wave Fountain*: blue sparks or turquoise, Pacific or South Pacific? Take your pick.

Or yes, we could stick to the same old basics: *United, Indivisible.* Instead of seals of approval, yes, we could just keep fireworks for all.

HOW TO CARVE A PUMPKIN

It's fair to say I write a lot about our built and natural environments. And right now, late October, I can't help thinking that holidays fall into those categories too. We need them instinctively—to mark the change of seasons, wish and give, commemorate and look forward—but we also make them up, creating or inheriting celebrations. Built and natural.

Take Halloween: It isn't generically American, but many people don't know this. It came north out of Mexico, and west with the Irish across the Atlantic; two historically reviled groups—wrong looks, wrong speech, wrong religion—but throw their celebrations in the microwave of marketing, and *presto*: Halloween is mainstream and everyone's carving jack-o-lanterns.

There's a reason for that, an origin story about where jack-o-lanterns come from. It's about Jack, Ireland's wildest carouser, and it goes like this:

Jack was a bad man, always swearing and brawling. He whirled through women like a lust tornado, pegged rocks at all the cops and priests, so everyone knew that Jack was going to hell.

But Jack was a talker too. He had the gift of persuasion and storytelling, and when the devil came, Jack promised that he could change.

"Just a year's reprieve," he bargained. "I'll quit with my pocket knife and stabbing the asses of my enemies, and these hands won't be for fists anymore but for bringing alms to the nuns on Sunday, and no more getting into underskirts and romping away behind the hedgerows," until finally the devil was impressed and believed him and agreed.

A barrel of lies, of course. Jack went on the same as ever. The year rolled by full of pints and fighting until one night the devil reappeared.

"Mr. Devil," says Jack, "I'm sorry for deceiving you. I'll come along quiet now, I promise. But couldn't I have a last supper before we go? I'm starvin' famished. No? Then how about one last apple, though I'll need you to climb up and reach it for me—that one on the branch near the top should do it—on account of my knuckles are swollen from punching, and my ankle's nearly broken after leaping out a woman's window."

Now, the devil can't believe it, but sure enough he's climbing, shimmying out on a waving branch, when *slash, slash* there's Jack with his pocket knife, carving a cross in the tree trunk, so the devil's trapped, he's stuck and ridiculous because he can't get down past that cross, so Jack's away to the pub again and waving fare-thee-well.

No one can out-talk Death though, and Jack died one day, as we all will. Of course, heaven was as closed as a treasure chest, but it turned out hell was too. The devil never forgave him for his trick that night and sent Jack away into exile in the cold and dark of space. A terrible doom, an endless emptiness, walking and walking through eternity alone.

It was a pretty sad plight, and the devil knew it, so first he gave Jack a bit of hellfire for comfort.

"Get out your clever pocket knife," he said, "and that turnip in your pocket. Carve it out hollow and have yourself this coal, some light for your journeying."

And that's how Jack became Jack of the Lantern.

Of course, Americans have traded in turnips for pumpkins. They're bigger and softer and easier to carve. Most of us don't remember this part, though: Those lanterns are to light the way for the dead to come visit the living, to return each All Hallows Eve and enjoy the food and drink we set out for them. It isn't just custom, it's ceremony.

Trick-or-treating isn't the same, I know. It isn't the best that we can do. But oh well, kids love it, so don't duck out and be gone that night, your house left empty and dark. Stay home and pass out sugar in abundance. In exchange for agreeing to do that, I'll give you these three things in return:

First, humpback whales are amazing. There's a good chance to see them in Monterey Bay. But it's the smell I actually remember most, hanging in the air after they've gone back under, something nostril-searing and ancient and you can't pass through it like a curtain, a blowhole smell of Ocean-Dead, a smell of considerable size. Second is Rainier cherries. You should definitely eat them. And no, Bings are no substitute. Try to do this in Grandview or Zillah since Mt. Rainier looks different from the east side. Short of that, though, a grocery store will do. Buy pounds, fill up; they're here and gone like orchard lightning. And third is Miles Davis's *My Funny Valentine Live*, his group with George Coleman not Coltrane. Those first haunting notes Miles carves with his trumpet—they'll hollow you out and put a light inside. They're like the prayers that Jack should have offered...

May the road rise up to meet you.

Toda la tierra es mi corazon.

Amen.

SOCIAL STUDIES

My kid is twelve, and he's reading *Frankenstein*, and he's down to the final ten pages, the part where Victor's giving a speech to Captain Walton's crew—calling them cowards because they want to turn south when the ice breaks—and Quentin groans, "Oh come on, Frankenstein, all you care about is getting to go after your beast." He can read the guy like an X-ray.

Could I have done that when I was twelve? I don't know. I was a reader myself, but nothing like this book. In fact, my own clearest memory of seventh grade doesn't have to do with literature at all. It's Mrs. Beulah Felhoffer: Social Studies and Current Events.

The jump in expectations from 6th grade to junior high wasn't the issue. I was diligent and grade-scared. Plus, my dad taught high school Civics, History, Psychology/Sociology, Contemporary World Problems, so I had a ringer in my corner if I needed one. And this was May 19, 1980, the day after Mt. St. Helen's erupted: ash burying all of eastern Washington; the Cowlitz River strangled by wiped-out forests and mud; a man named Harry Truman entombed in his cabin on the shores of Spirit Lake; and even my hometown, Puyallup, which sat north of the ash plume and away from the path of the jet stream, was everywhere dusted in volcano color. Incredible. I brought in the whole damn *News Tribune* and figured it was a slam-dunk A.

I got an F.

My dad was never one of those parents primed to skirmish with anyone who failed to appreciate his offspring, but this time he did ask to meet with my teacher and came home thinking that the woman might really be insane. Apparently she'd told him an acceptable current event was "something important. Like a story on the moon landing." Hers was a rare definition of *current.*

Around this same time, I took an I.Q. test, something my dad was using with his college-prep seniors. Some professor, I guess, had put it together, intending to give white people a jolt. I'd always liked this sort of quizzing. Take Lucky Lager, for instance: If your parents chose Lucky in bottles over cans of Oly or Rainier, it meant you got to solve these puzzles on the inside of the caps; very cool. Anyway, the test had ten or so questions sort of like this:

Duke Ellington is to piano, as...

a) Billie Holiday is to ballads,

b) Miles Davis is to trumpet.

c) Lester Young is to tenor sax.

d) Dizzy Gillespie is to trumpet.

If you're thinking *You've got to be kidding me*, then you're halfway right.

And even if you're thinking that you're hip to this, you're probably still a little unsure, maybe trying to work out the logic: "Do I base my answer on the musical era (Billie Holiday), or on the style (it's swing, so Lester Young), or is it just their names/nicknames beginning with the letter D?" No, no, and no. The only acceptable answer to the question is B. Why?—because Miles, like Duke, was a composer (not Dizzy; he didn't sight read) as well as immortal on trumpet like Ellington was immortal on keys. My test score marked me as illiterate, which didn't feel fair—culturally specific referents aren't basic common knowledge—and that was the point.

And it brings me back to *Frankenstein*. Victor thinks that he's been doomed by Fate, but he's wrong. He's just cocooned in privilege—

a) Moneyed?

b) Male?

c) Racial?

d) All of the above?

—which isn't the only reason for his ethical near-sightedness, but it doesn't help.

Worse, as Quentin will soon find out while reading the last ten pages, Victor doesn't learn, and if personifying Prideful/Rash Disaster doesn't teach you a clarifying lesson, nothing will.

Two hundred years ago, Mary Shelley knew this. She knew it at the age of eighteen. I'd rather cast my vote for her than most of the office-seekers these days. Imagine the headline *that* would generate: "Illegal Alien's Ghost Wins Election."

I could mail it to Mrs. Felhoffer and flunk again.

TRIGONOMETRY

I've lived most of my life in Washington and Utah. Throw in all the driving I've done in Oregon, Idaho, Wyoming, and Montana, and it feels like a head start on looking at things. All that size. Everywhere. Iconic and mythic.

And it's myths that actually matter. I can say, "In the Old Songs about Washington, salmon nested in trees," and it isn't untrue. Not in a myth. Not in a story. Not even in fact, it turns out if you think of tree roots as underground branches, think of nesting as letting go (like sleep, just forever), transforming, becoming nitrogen.

What happens—I learned this a few days ago—is that most of the salmon the bears take from rivers aren't just eaten right there. A lot get carried into the woods, and I love that, love thinking of bears as these clawed and massive accidental gardeners whose table scraps fertilize forests. Trading this for a pipeline down the coast of B.C.'s Inner Channel seems like something only the thoughtless and heart-blind would do. As in, Earth - Bears - Woods = No, no, no. We don't need fewer archetypes and less empathy, we need more...

Back when I was in high school, we started at 7:45, which meant starting in blackness during winter. The 49th parallel. The days are short. They start late and end early. My first-period class was Trigonometry, and one time out the back window I saw a thin line of light appear and outline Mt. Rainier. Suddenly there, an orange tracing, a black silhouette.

Another minute and the sun was rising, and this was Washington, overcast, the whole sky ceilinged, so the sun split into streaks of color—pinks and reds and whatever—on the undersides of the clouds. Then things filled in and blended, then the sun was halfway up behind the mountain, and the scene out the window was just another January morning.

I think I got a B+ in Trig that year, or maybe even an A. But those three minutes are the only part I remember.

ADDITION + SUBTRACTION

If there's a Nobel Prize for mountains, it should go to Mt. Rainier. Before I tell you why, though, here's something I learned about Tempe, Arizona. My friend Brian was explaining about buying a house there. "What you do," he said, "is find one you like and then ask the neighbors about scorpions." Some blocks are seething with them, some blocks aren't, and scorpions don't care about poured foundations. Set concrete on ground a thousand scorpions have been calling home and no amount of flooring, framing, and wishing is going to keep them out. Your house will be Scorpion City.

We should remember better than we usually do that details like this are what count. Forget the number of bathrooms, the stainless steel gas range. Go knock on doors along your maybe street and ask, "Scorpions? How many? How many times a day?" Call it the World's Strange Mathematics.

Now, about Mt. Rainier. I know one of the best places to see it: from a leftover scrap of the valley I grew up in. There are two ways to get from Puyallup to Tacoma, Pioneer Way and River Road. One is winding and the other one's straight, and ironically River Road is the straight one, so usually I'd cut over. Two smaller roads let you do that, the second one running through these strawberry fields. I want to say the farm is Van Lierop's, but I know that isn't right. Picha's! That's the family's name. And hallelujah that their farm is still a farm. How rare is that these days? Too rare. Anyway, because it's a farm—muddy, open land by the wide, wide acre—there's still a view: this ecstatic corridor with Mt. Rainier at the end of it, giant. You could parcel the view into subdivisions and sell it nine hundred times, become a zillionaire, only you can't, not without making it worthless. See, you need that *nothing-in-the-way-ness* for the view to be the view: a snow-capped volcano that just keeps rising.

Fourteen.

Thousand.

Feet.

Developers might see it differently, but they'd be wrong. My friend Jamie put it perfectly: "Mt. Rainier gets overlooked in a traffic jam. Even though you actually have more time to look at it." How much more so in a human jam of identical three-bedroom boxes? More than I want to think about, so I won't. I'd rather wonder what the mountain is thinking.

When it's looking down over the valley of us, out west toward Puget Sound, I bet it thinks our strawberry fields are an odd but glad addition. Our sprawl and neon graffiti not so much.

SEVEN BIRDS

Northeast of Salt Lake City:

Higher up the Wasatch, just outside of Heber, you can see these fledgling eagles learning to fly. They take turns swooping, landing in the meadow, letting loose an eagle *shriek* or *Amen*. And no, I can't do impressions, can't name each bone in their wings, but I can tell you for certain that the grassland below them has mice, and a few more years before it's gone. Become in-fill. The suburbs covering the valley. The suburbs like a new sort of glacier made of plastic and cul-de-sac tar.

The Outskirts of Sydney:

I'll admit it was thirty years ago, so by now things might

have changed, but the only McDonald's I remember is this one in the suburbs of Sydney, Australia. Their hamburgers didn't come with ketchup—you had to buy that extra—and they didn't call it ketchup:

"Oh, you mean sauce?"

"Yeah, sure. Tomato sauce. How much for that?"

The rest was the usual—the uniforms, the furniture, even the straws—despite the Date Line and the upside-downness of the hemisphere and the alien patterns of the constellations, and we'd driven on the wrong side to get there, and I was the one with the accent, and the teenage guys called the teen girls "birds."

But McDonald's was the same.

In Our Garden:

I was out weeding the garden. My wife Jen was cleaning the garage.

"Hey, you might want to see this," I said. "There are quail."

The male was nearby, just a couple feet away, calling out and ignoring me, and the female was three plots behind me, ignoring him.

"She's got chicks," Jen said.

They were chittering under the sunflowers, probably eating the seeds since there are lots, more and more each year, more than the birds can finish, so some take root, grow back, the first green action in April...*volunteers*—that's what it's called when they do that: plants that you don't have to plant. Look around: sunflowers everywhere, leaning over the fence between the day-care playground and the vacant lot, and jumping from front yards to medians, then on down the block...a take-over, sure, but with waving.

And never that same kind of yellow as parking lot stripes.

Purdy, Washington:

I, too, would like a cabin there, with a footpath down to the oyster-shell beach, where some days, looking for hermit crabs, I might see herons come gliding...Great Blue, their eight-foot wingspans, taking fish, or not, from this narrow end of the inlet; either way.

What an arrangement of angles.

Who can beat that?

Next Door to My House:

My neighbor told me there are people who still eat doves. I don't know if I believe him.

He's got a box in his tree for kestrels, though, so probably.

2017:

There's that scene—remember?—at the end of *Jurassic Park*, where the ones not eaten are rescued, and Dr. Grant looks out the helicopter window, smiling at a flight-line of pelicans, his hypothesis confirmed: *Dinosaurs aren't extinct. They just escaped into adaptation.*

And so could we. At least I think so, because I'm not Scott Pruitt. I didn't drop in from Oklahoma to mismanage the Environmental Protection Agency.

The Kitchen Counter Where I'm Writing This:

It's almost time for another Thanksgiving, when the President will pardon a turkey; it's tradition.

Another is saying what you're thankful for, so here goes:

To the birds who make our neighborhoods their neighborhoods as well, who lend their songs and *ya-honks* to the morning. And to seagulls—what good is a shoreline without you? The sky would be missing its dancers, and the wind a one-note orchestra. To blue jays yelling at people from fence posts; and roosters doing your farm-strut; and the childhood robins of my Washington, constant as the rain. To you hawks above our freeways who leave roadkill-picking to magpies—you don't wait for an after-life, you soar right now, seeing much farther than we do. To peacocks forever looking Mardi Gras; and to owls, you Ministers of Silence; and to you, the birds in my future, let me say thanks.

And thanks yesterday.

And thanks again tomorrow.

May all of you be well.

ENVIRONMENTAL STUDIES

Washington:

Washington's state bird is the goldfinch, but as a kid growing up there I always thought that seemed wrong. Robins you saw everywhere, especially after rain, hopping around and unspooling worms from the lawn—night crawlers long as a shoelace—but goldfinches? Almost never. They were mostly just pictures in books.

Utah:

So imagine my surprise last month when I spotted a goldfinch in my Salt Lake City yard. No, two...no, three...wait, there's another one. Four. Parent with fledglings? Boyfriend and girlfriends? I wasn't sure. One had vivid feathers, black and yellow. The other three were more muted, with coloring less like exclamation points.

I'd been reading the Friday *Salt Lake Tribune*, skimming the recaps of politics, and was heading out to clear the wind-snapped branches from the yard, and there they were, riding these wire-thin tensile stems that rise up out of a plant near the sidewalk, see-sawing on the ends and eating the flowers, or maybe just the bugs on the flowers, I don't know.

What I do know is they didn't give a crap about Donald Trump.

Political Climate:

"First-ism"; trans., "isolationism." Always forever hollering about this: banning Muslims, rounding up aliens (their word, not mine), talk of shakin' down NATO for "protection money," reneging on international trade pacts, and tweets about reneging on more. And so on.

A lot gets said about the ethical/economic sinkhole this will cause, but I don't hear much about it being bad for the environment, and it is. The environment isn't American, isn't an our-side/your-side attitude. I mean, who's going to work with us on long-term fixes if we've traded away good will for an unfounded claim on a baseball hat?

Utah:

The day I saw those goldfinches was another in a long stretch of 100+ degrees. And there were algal blooms too, turning water into warnings, signs going up along shorelines, basically saying: STAY AWAY OR THIS WILL KILL YOU.

Add air-pollution advisories, and other examples year 'round, and we should be concerned.

U.S.A:

Each state knows what I'm talking about. We can't deport rising temperatures. We can't turn our backs on the water and the air.

My House:

I'm dodging a moth while I write this, which strikes me as kind of funny. It's drinking the condensation, I think, off the can of Rainier beside me on the table, then berzerking its way from lamp to lamp, then coming back to flap in my face, in my ear, then finally land in the crook of my elbow. It's as graceless as those goldfinches were graceful, and I'm glad I got to see them. They aren't commonplace in Utah, but even the worst ornithologist would never call them "aliens." And this moth on my beer is a nuisance, yes, but I like it way more than I like Jeff Sessions.

Political Climate:

Did you see that? Somehow it seeped in again—politics like Thought Smog—when all I wanted was to offer you a poem. It's environmental, and it goes like this:

THE MOTHER OF THE MOUNTAINS

If a mama bear gets angry, imagine the Mother of the Mountains.
Mess with Her children, She'll dust off an avalanche;
step out of line, She'll realign your bones.
She's a blue-eyed beauty,
and the mountains have their Mother's eyes: deep lakes.

Gaze into them, you'll see their thoughts like fish—
quick schools, slow rainbows—look deeper,
and you'll learn to dream like a stone.
What does She feed them? Rain for breakfast.
Anything else? She peels them the sun for lunch.
And at night? Big helpings of quiet,
then the Mother of the Mountains sings them to sleep with snow.
The trees are Her grandkids; She brings them birds to play with.
Whenever it's their birthday, She gives them an owl
'cause though She's a blue-eyed beauty, She's still kind.
Even soft ... even fragile ...
Wolves howl to Her to show their gratitude. What about you?

ENVIRONMENTAL CLEAN-UP

Salt Lake City:

It made the newspaper here—this weed that's swallowed the foothills and taken hold in places inaccessible to mountain goats, this weed that you can't cut back because its sap is a milky burning poison, this weed that burned my hands and burned my face when I wiped the sweat off; you have to pull it out, uproot it, every stem like a toxic livewire: myrtle spurge.

It blisters you deep red and ugly, and its name is fitting, as if the olden-days botanist who dubbed it was a linguist too. Go ahead and say it out loud once: myrtle *spurge*. It sounds as lousy as it is.

2018:

I'm not going to hunt down citations for this. I've been weeding and weeding all week, and the internet feels like that too—weeds you can't pull out except by typing—and just hearing it once on National Public Radio was bad enough. Mick Mulvaney, the interim head of the Consumer Financial Protection Bureau, decided, like some kind of Dickens character, to stop enforcing the laws against defrauding people with student loans. Before Mulvaney showed up last November, this bureau had gotten back $750 million, some of it for veterans on the G.I. Bill, but not anymore. Now it's under the umbrella of Consumer Education, and instead of claw-backs and criminal investigations these CFPB employees have to busy themselves making pamphlets on things like diligence, pluck, and the keys to personal budgeting.

Mick Mulvaney's House:

OPERATOR: 9-1-1; please state your emergency.

MULVANEY: I've been robbed. Somebody broke into my house.

OPERATOR: Are they still there now, or are you alone?

MULVANEY: No, I'm alone.

OPERATOR: And what was taken?

MULVANEY: All my money. Thousands and thousands and thousands. And my time, and belief in justice, and—

OPERATOR: I understand you're upset, sir. Someone's on their way right—

MULVANEY: Thank God. Thanks for taking this seriously.

OPERATOR: They're on their way over with some pamphlets for Tae Kwan Do and burglar alarms.

Two Days Before Mother's Day:

And here's John Kelly, the White House Chief of Staff, reasoning with NPR. They're on the topic of immigrants and yanking their kids away.

He's saying the majority of immigrants aren't criminals, but they don't "assimilate into our modern society." And they're "rural" and "don't speak English" and only have a sixth-grade education. He's saying that they "don't have skills"; and anyway, the law's the law; plus, the "name of the game is deterrence." Which leads the reporter—John Burdette, I think—to add that, yeah, but taking their kids might also be cruel, so now John Kelly's reassuring him that it's not. He's saying the kids, some of them toddlers and babies, will be "put into foster care or whatever."

Those were his words: *or whatever*. You can look it up.

Ireland:

My last name is Irish. And so are Mulvaney's and Kelly's. And if I could revoke their Irishness, I would.

Back when their great-grandparents were going through lifetimes of English-made suffering, I doubt they passed their days with thoughts like this: *Just live. Survive. And one day your kids will have kids who have kids who can do this to someone else.*

Salt Lake City:

Nettles, thistles, knapweed, dandelions, crabgrass, cheat-grass, purslane, mallow, something called tall fescue, and something else called prostrate knotweed, and puncturevines (*Tribulus terrestris*, probably the Latin name for "Land of Stress and Tribulation," which it is. Step barefoot on their thorns, for instance. Or try to ride a bike anywhere. Or sit on the grass; I dare you. Or let your pets go walking on the Earth), and of course myrtle spurge, like twelve new disciples.

Disciples of Plague and Malediction.

Washington, DC:

John Kelly, Mick Mulvaney, the whole Trump phantasmagoria: myrtle spurge.

TRUTH > THE NEWS

The End of March 2019:

I saw my friend Nano. That doesn't happen often. He lives way down in Cedar City, and I'm in Salt Lake. I saw him up in Portland, Oregon, at the mega writer's conference. Nano said, "I've been reading some more about your dad online. He sounds like a really good dude."

Which was unexpected, nice to hear, and yes he was.

Making Lists:

My dad had a list of things that he'd been working on (so Capricorn), and it was done: the house was packed, the house was on the market, and the new Methodist retirement community that he and my mom were moving to was ready. After years of hassles over permits and inertia, it was built. And he'd found the right car to buy, the right one for getting in and out. His breathing had been an issue for years—low oxygen, and no fixing it—so he had to think carefully about stepping and exertion, every action and distance like a new kind of necessary math. And now it was done.

My mom's new phone was set up.

The car was out there parked in the garage.

And a dozen other details were finished, and then to bed, where these were his next-to-last words: "Well, that's the whole list."

Then he asked my mom to hold him. Then he breathed a while more. And then he stopped.

April 3, 2019:

So that was a year ago. It's been a year's worth of news since then, a whole pile-up of idiot cruelty out of DC, or New York, or Mar-a-Lago, or somewhere, wherever the self-pleased Biped-in-Chief goes next.

My dad wouldn't like it.

Nobody should.

Trump's backtrack to shovel more hate at Puerto Rico, and his hate for the immigrants stuck in El Paso, and his insults to Congressman Elijah Cummings—Trump is the worst.

And oh yeah, the environment. Always the environment. The environment and Russia are the two things he lies about most. They're like the latitude and longitude of his ocean-sized lying, and the rest is just a leaky faucet that never stops. *LIE/drip. LIE/drip. LIE/drip. LIE/drip. LIE.* And yet he's got an audience...

...Poets Don't,

at least not usually. Still, we never stop trying.

It would be helpful to know that someone's noticing, that poems don't drop like pebbles down a well and disappear. Maybe they ripple a bit, maybe echo and change the taste of the water, make the moss on the nearby stones a little greener; that would be nice. I'd like to add that to my résumé: Greener-Up of Living Things, Echo Riding on the Water.

It depends, I know, on what I write about and how well I do it. But anything, even this fable I'm folding like an origami pretzel, is better than a tweet:

THE THREE LITTLE PIGS

I've never liked this story.
It says two out of three pigs are lazy.
It says wolves don't hunt,
they huff and puff—Come on,
that's concocted by some brick-house people
safe at home,
tucked snugly in the afterglow,
in their choice of news that tells them
bricks are bricks,
and sticks reflect a lack of effort,
and straw
is the fault of Puerto Rico; they forget why.
Just don't be the Brick Pig's problem.
If you'd rather have landscapes with caribou herds
instead of pit mines,
try to want less; what're you,
a wolf or something? You think clean air
grows on trees?

Don't come asking for asylum
or they'll huff and puff.

April 3—Thinking About Making a List:

Things, of course, need doing. Even today.

Like getting some groceries. Jen and I and Jameson were up in Portland, as I said, and now we're back, and we haven't felt like shopping. Who wants to shift gears? Who wants to get off the plane and swing by Whole Foods, or Smith's, or whatever other grocery store? Not us.

Anyway, I was walking back from the mailbox when this thought popped into my head: Take them out to The Old Spaghetti Factory. Problem solved.

That was where my dad used to take us, over to the one in Tacoma, somewhere up the hill, around a corner, then down a diagonal (all of the streets in Tacoma are like that; the city's old, a port city, its pavement laid down over cobblestones that were set down on top of the donkey tracks), and we were there. And I always loved going.

You can think I'm wrong if you want to, but that thought popping into my head was from my dad. He's still here helping me. Like an echo. Like a ripple.

My dad's still here with an answer so much greener and living than the news.

IN THE BEGINNING WAS A RIVER

People who know me know this: I don't pretend to be an expert on the legal codes of New Zealand.

But back in March something happened there that keeps on running through my mind. Their House of Representatives, which must be a whole bunch different than ours, passed a bill giving human rights to the Whanganui River. How's that for treatment of a natural resource? Pretty good.

And what I keep thinking—now that a river can claim personhood and dignity—is, what do I want to suggest for human rights next?

Probably stars. They deserve to be noticed. Once a month

we'll have darkness by decree. We'll have twelve new ways to look up, a dozen needed oases.

And Puget Sound, of course. Whether seen from a ferry or not. Whether or not it's sundown on Seattle's million windows so the skyline is mirroring gold-orange, rose, and red, and the Olympic Mountains are both in front of you and behind you, and seagulls ride rivers of updraft, and this time and place and wind should be vested with rights.

The trees near Crescent City too—they're older than Christianity. I'll call each redwood a cathedral, drinking fog, which truly is Holy Water.

The snowmelt I drank in an ice cave: rights.

Those ghost-conversations of coyotes: rights.

That soul-blown sound of a train at night—part love, part loss, and part Coltrane—couldn't be more human, with the human right to quiet, so that everyone who needs to hear can hear.

And what about you? Isn't there a lakeshore somewhere? Or a night in some December? Or a time you saw some pronghorn and were doubly surprised—first by their nearness, then a second time by how they leapt away: too squat to be bounding like that? Isn't there a long-distance drive you've taken with a good enough reason at the end of it? Or a kiss that lives in your memory, that goes on rivering and rivering? Or a view from the porch of a lightning storm coursing the sky?

Anyway, it's April, soon to be summer in Utah, where most aren't yelling and opposed to helping refugees. Most don't think it's okay to zero them out, leave them trapped in their national horrors.

In New Zealand they've granted more rights than that to a river, which ought to be an elemental lesson.

Here's hoping it flows all the way from there to D.C.

II.

WINE IS RAIN IN TRANSLATION

POETRY

The poem is a shapeshifter animal, a trickster.
One minute, it's a sailfish. The next, it's a hook.
One night, it's an alley cat, urgent to get you outdoors,
get you on the fire escape and screaming. Another, it sleeps.
I remember there was a great migration—poems soaring home.
And I remember, too, when they used to thunder like trains,
crushing the grass.
I watched as the herd turned into crickets ... then rain ...
then into kids in the backyard, running for the house
before the raindrops turned into hail, and while I watched
I smelled my dinner burning. Clever trick.
"Well, what's the good in that?" Not much.

"Then what the hell's it want?" I don't know—to astonish
like leaves do in autumn. To hope, I guess,
it says one small thing that lasts.

I'd prefer to leave it at that, to add nothing, since going on now means reducing the poem to an epigram, as if prose were really the bigger-stakes work, and I don't want to concede that. But back in mid-September my friend Joe Roberts wrote me a note that I've been thinking about ever since.

He said, "I have a question for you. I've been struggling to come up with a purpose for poetry as it is, as opposed to prose. What makes poetry's purpose distinctive?"

Thank you, Joe. It's nice being thought of as a guy who might have an answer.

On the one hand, I'm not sure poems have to have a purpose. I mean, I'd rather have lamps be lamps and let poems be the occasional genie. On the other hand, I know that's ridiculous. Poems *do* have purposes, lots of them, and I shouldn't avoid adding my thoughts about what those purposes are just because doing so takes some work. I know this won't be my final answer—there will be days ahead when I think of others, then others after that—but here goes: Joe said he'd been reading *Spring and All* (William Carlos Williams). He said Williams' ideas were pretty good. He said, "The definition I pulled from him is that prose is meant to serve the emotions and be representational. Poetry is meant to serve the imagination and create something truly new. It's not a mirror to hold up to nature; it is an addition to nature, a 'crystallization of the imagination.'"

Now, I love Williams by the acre, the square mile, but I'm going to say I think he's probably wrong about that one. Take Faulkner's *Go Down, Moses*. It's prose not poetry, and it's truly new. And that's just one example. In fact, it's the first that popped into my head.

Here's another: Pick any of a dozen albums by Bob Dylan; what's happening seems both true and new to me, and also different than a poem, or even a whole book of poems, since there's the added interplay of voice and instruments to go along with whatever story or character or philosophical headlock he's turned into lyrics.

No, probably the rightest part of Williams' idea is the "crystallization" thing. Faulkner gives us whole caves full of stalactites, stalagmites, bats, pooling water old as Original Sin, and also crystals; yet love that as much as you want, you can't wear it around your neck. Same with Dylan. Sure, he's bardic, but how long do you think it took the roadies to unload and set up for every concert on, say, his Rolling Thunder Revue tour in 1975? What's different (distinct) about poems, I think, isn't fancy. It's that they're short.

I said this once to Tony Weller, a bookseller in Salt Lake City. At first he thought I was a spluttering dunce, or just being lazy about the question. But I halfway talked him around to my point of view: Poems are short, even when halfway behaving like narratives, even when sharing a compact story. They're crystallized: Life's psalm, Heart's wind chimes, Guts' tattoo. I'm saying—and yes, I started this by saying the opposite ("Do I contradict myself? / Very well then I contradict myself, / I am large, I contain multitudes"; Walt Whitman)—I'm saying that the distinction of poetry is *its ability to be epigrammatic*. You can carry a poem inside you like a talisman because you can remember it completely, start to finish, word for word. And it doesn't need accompaniment, just you reciting the lines and the rhythms, all its images and meanings, meanings you might start to paraphrase then decide that you don't really need to after all.

LYNX MUSIC

The lynx knows all about quiet,
his ears grown long to hear more of it.
He sharpens his claws on the trunk of it,
hunts silence,
carries it home. And his paws
ghost over snowdrifts,
and lakes are asleep
under ice sheets,
and the stars seem frozen
like an orchestra, waiting to begin ...
has anyone seen the conductor?
Where has she gone in her night tuxedo?
The lynx looks ready to tell us something,
but only in the speech of violins.

EVOLUTION

My friend Jason asked me what I thought of a poem he'd just written. He was on a train somewhere, headed back to Brooklyn—this was through email—and I told him I liked it but might change a couple phrases.

He said, "Thanks but I'm thinking I need to blow the whole thing up and make it much weirder," that it was too much like "the imitation of a poem rather than an actual poem."

That's the sort of savvy stuff I'm used to from him, and it made me start running through my own Inventory of the Weird, like I'm lab-testing his hypothesis.

It checks out. For instance, the movie *Tin Cup* was on TV yesterday, and my favorite part is still when Roy and his friend (and caddy) Romeo are getting out of Roy's old convertible Cadillac, and Romeo tells him, "I only got one rule, boss, and that's never bet money that you don't have on a dog race with an ex-girlfriend who happens to be a stripper, and you broke that rule, Holmes. Now you're gonna have to be sweet to her." This dialogue isn't plot-centric at all. It's just there. Weirdness that levitates.

Another example: I spent two nights in Hamilton, Montana, as a guest being taken care of by strangers. One night I stepped out onto the back stoop and almost into a porcupine. It was there, maybe a foot away, eating out of the dog dish. I stood still, and thought about stillness, until it finally settled its quills back down and plodded off between the apple trees. Now, who cares what happened on the other night?

Or take New York City, where Jason lives, and not porcupines but Frank O'Hara. O'Hara's got a poem ("Personal Poem") about hanging out with his friend Leroi Jones, and he mentions the construction on all the corners and girders of Manhattan, saying, "If / I ever get to be a construction worker / I'd like to have a silver hat please." Who's he talking to—himself? the reader? some imaginary god of hard hat dispersal? It doesn't matter. It's a goofball outburst of weirdness.

I think what I mean—what Jason meant too—is that weirdness can also be an evolution.

If you don't believe me, go and look at a moose. Did you know they can close their nostrils and stay underwater like these algae-grazing submarines? You don't get weirder than an angler fish, but it works. What's got more style, a cow or a longhorn?

It's the same thing with writing. Weird is good.

GRAVITATIONAL PULL

So it's December, smack dab between *What are you thankful for?* and New Year's resolutions, but those things aren't on my mind at all. What I'm actually thinking about is the moon, the way it's up there pulling.

I know it's pulled me many times, especially when it's full. Once it even pulled my friend Jason and me at the same time, same direction, and not because we're both the same zodiac sign. He's Virgo; I'm Cancer.

This was back in our student days in South Louisiana, south of I-10, south of Carencro, south of Prejean's Restaurant—food so good I wish I could order up and eat my own memories—south of the track: Evangeline Downs, the horses, reading the race form and placing your bets. We hadn't planned this, hadn't driven there together. I just went, and started up the bleacher stairs, and there's Jason wearing the same expression I am, like *You too? What the hell?*

Did we win? Lose? I don't know; probably we broke about even. The thing I remember is the parking lot after, when we rounded the corner and couldn't miss it—this full moon, bright orange, about as big as Jupiter, looking like it's perched on the cypress trees a hundred yards away. It was one of those moments, rare and wonderful, when you catch yourself pausing for a microsecond, and I said, "Wow," and Jason said, "No wonder we came here." Case closed.

Maybe the moon's been on my mind because it seems to live pretty near where I do. Like some beautiful, crazy neighbor. When it's time, it rises low and huge just behind the Wasatch Mountains, and maybe even out of them, from some secret valley or cold river canyon. Anyway, looking across my backyard, it doesn't feel impossible.

I don't have a grand point I'm making here or anything. I'd rather just offer up one of my moon poems and hope it orbits in your thoughts awhile. If it pulls you from low tide to high tide, that would be nice.

THERE'S STILL SO MUCH TO LEARN ABOUT THE MOON:

where it comes from; and if it misses home;
and why there's just the one, not three or four;
and why some nights you barely notice it
but others it can break your heart, so full
there isn't any room inside for what—
beauty? memory? the push and pull
of loss, of losing what was never yours

to begin with? Meanwhile, we go charting tides
and turning pages of our calendars.
Telescopes get aimed, and side by side
a boy might ask his father if the moon
feels lonely. Side by side, two people sleep,
moonlight spread across the bed ... soft, silver,
but cold: So they'll hold close. So they'll keep warm.

WINE IS RAIN IN TRANSLATION

Wine is rain in translation. And corkscrews are lines in translation. And glasses are sand in translation, sometimes on stems. How cool would it be if we could plant them, watch them turn and lean toward the sun?

I've been thinking about translation on and off for about a month, ever since *Terrain.org* published four Icelandic poems. There was something about the way they fit on the screen so you couldn't see the English without scrolling down, and I decided I didn't want to. Not until I'd tried my own "translations" first.

My friend Rick suggested this years ago: working out approximate versions in English based solely on the way another language looks...the pattern of letters, and how you might pronounce them, and so on. Having no clue about the original was his only rule.

I definitely didn't. To me the title of the first poem looked like "Origami Journey," assuming you could flip the adjective the way you would in Spanish. I dug that idea (*What's an origami journey?*), but the opening line, which looked like "Kari's grandmother," hooked me more, so that's where I started. Then the second line had something close to "put some scribbles here." And a long word (a kenning?) in the fourth line looked a lot like "it's-spring-again" all run together.

It didn't matter that none of this was going to be right. Not literally. Literally, the poem is about not stepping on beetles. That wasn't the sort of translation I was up to though, and I can't imagine Magnús Sigurdsson would mind. He might even see it the same way I do: Sometimes it's not bad to bend things. The first slam dunk bent the sky and the future. Billie Holiday bent songs. And bending a straight line around and around amounts to something that can uncork wine. All of us ought to try bending more. So I did:

"ART IS SUCH A GOOD JOURNEY"

Kari's grandmother used to tell us,
"Put some scribbles there—
a million begonias.
And now it's spring again, blooming. Yes."
Not scuba,
not yoga,
not for her,
but she could make you young-eyed
when teaching you to paint.

"Orange pinwheels, try it,
that's sunlight,
that's Mama Eggs." And my favorite,
what I'll never forget:
"Don't ever put your vision on
like shoes, my darlings. We're traveling,
not making doormats."

POETRY AS COLLAGE

"WHAT ARE YOUR SKILLS?"

Every year at Sea School
we were taught that glaciers purr
and ice floes, huge
below the surface, were sunning cats.
Call ours a failed education.
If it makes you feel better,
call our hymns under night skies
cracked.
But for thirteen years
we sailed on bluer water.

And all of us know well
how to arch our backs.

My favorite American artist is Romare Bearden. I especially love his collages. One called *Mill Hand's Lunch Bucket*, for example, led August Wilson (love him too) to write his play *Joe Turner's Come and Gone*. If I remember right, Wilson said the haunted-looking figure seated in the center became his character Harold Loomis.

For me, though, it's another figure coming down the stairs who makes the biggest impact. Out the window we see the dragon-fire and industry-teeth of smokestacks, and it's clear that this man is on his way to work there, and he's a normal-sized man, and the lunchbox on the boarding house table is normal-sized, but the man's hand is huge: his hunger/need/soul so much bigger than the opportunities life as a Black man in a mill town will provide. That's a powerful commentary. It's Social-Realism, only to get there Bearden ditches the realism.

I try to do that too, preferring myth, for instance, to confessional modes and sticking to the facts. And in the case of these two poems, I'm almost working in collage.

For example, "What Are Your Skills?" is my guess about what Magnús Sigurdsson's title "Vatnaskil" might be in English. And Icelandic words like "skolad," "mér," "purrt," "hugarfljótid," and "Undir nyjum / himni" became the fragments I combined into a Sea School, ice floes, purring cats, and hymns sung under night skies. Even better, my poem became a talking back to the ruling half of our country, and I swear that's because I set out to write while brain-blind. Instead of having an editorial subject, I had mystery and questions.

That's even truer of the next poem, "Are You Hungry?" At first I only had the title ("Vetrarhugar") and opening lines, "Pad hefur gránad / í fjöll," which looked to me like "Paul's grandfather fell." The bonus was that I don't know anyone named Paul, so I could just be an oracle:

"ARE YOU HUNGRY?"

Paul's grandfather fell
from his house in the air
when his dreaming turned to birds.
Sometimes it means you'll find a hawk's egg,
and others it just means listen to the river
saying, "Start in my stream
below the mountain's scar,
and ignore the bears around you.
Float still, a leaf, then find
momentum. You'll gain the whole sea."
Midnight visions
are a common kind of travel,
whether *just a journey*
or *a finding*.
But you can't peg orders, can't call the shots,
or dreams stall, lose power,
maybe drop you
from your tree house. You'll land
in an empty kitchen,
wanting bread.

These poems, of course, aren't actual collages. I know that. In an email, Magnús suggested an alternative term: "magnified or distorted collage, so to speak." That phrasing is fine with me, at least for now and unofficially, since a magnified tree would be a redwood, and distorted and magnified details are what I like about *Mill Hand's Lunch Bucket.*

Anyway, I hope these poems work similarly: zeroing in by distorting. And maybe they magnified a moment of your day.

LEARNING FROM BIRDS

There's a woodpecker two houses down from mine I could set my watch to if I wore a watch—8:11 a.m., four mornings in a row, up and down the light pole. *BAda DAda DAda DAda DA.* He's working in trochaic pentameter, jackhammer fast. Then pausing to listen, or maybe to mind-read tucked away termites, I don't know. He might be tuned to vibrations in the wood and using them for radar. Me, I try to catch the rhythm of a sentence, so maybe he's doing that too—woodpecker writing—and his pauses aren't listening *in* as much as listening *back*, then imagining forward.

Forward to what? In his case, bugs; and in my case, why that light pole? It's new, a replacement for the one knocked down, snapped off shin-high in a windstorm. But just because it's new to our street doesn't mean the *log* is new. It might have been dead or felled in the woods, the home of beetles for a decade, then a lumber crew brought it to the city, then they sold it to Lighting and Maintenance, who spiffed it up with an arm and a lamp so it's "new."

Though it isn't really. It just means our language has to hunt and stab, the same as any woodpecker. There's exactness and rightness in there somewhere, but you have to dig.

Perhaps he wants a vantage point since cats keep coming like phantoms. Or it's aesthetic, and he's drawn to straight lines like some are drawn to rhymes. It could be a matter of principle since trees are rooted in dignity, so to grab ahold and help yourself would just seem wrong; they're more than Someone's Future Firelight, or The Answer You Didn't Have to Work For. They're the planet's Librarians of Green, and this woodpecker knows it, and we should too.

I'm only guessing, of course. I haven't conducted an interview. There's a number in the phone book for Salt Lake City's urban forester, so I could call right now and ask, but I don't want to know. I mean, what if the answer's ordinary?—like *Light poles don't have bark you have to drill through. Think about all your own shortcuts.*

Speaking of which, I'm going to skip the conclusion and stick this fable here instead:

ORNITHOLOGY LESSONS

Because she loves a good rock slide,
a little geologic fanfare,
the blue jay taps at boulders with her beak,
quick chisels to get things rolling.

She turns her *Screek!* into a thunderclap
and lets the echo start the show: a cliff face
sheared away, a river
redirected,
a headache given to a mountain goat, and more—
the whole sky made to take notice...
What do we learn from this story?
Who thinks, "The color of the bird"?
You're right. And she looks fantastic with the sunlight
fitted around her like a dress.
The trees below rustle leaves in admiration.
Even their acorns are impressed.

WIN $300.00

I'll give a hundred bucks to the first person who correctly names the inventor of iambic pentameter. You can set aside reading this and call me with your answer (801-533-9887), but you have to do it now.

Three.

Two.

One.

No, it wasn't Shakespeare.

And no, not Chaucer either, though I've heard it said that he brought it back from Italy along with a copy of *The Decameron* and some horrible verse forms like the sestina.

I learned the answer years ago from an Irish poet named

Jim McAuley. I was in Spokane, taking classes in what used to be a bank. One classroom was actually the former vault, the huge door left there on its hinges. Crazy. And McAuley told us that iambic pentameter was just another thing the English stole from the Irish, which had my attention even before he got to the origin story, which was this: It came from the blacksmiths' shops. It was the practice of the master smith to use a smaller hammer—*tap*—to show his apprentice where the heavier blow should go—*bang*. It took five of these tap-bangs to shape a sword (tap BANG, tap BANG, tap BANG, tap BANG, tap BANG), which was a plausible explanation. More importantly, though, it was a perfect story because it also explains couplet rhymes: two sides to a sword (one side; flip; then the other), then back again with the metal to heat in the forge.

As for the specific Irish poet...by then I'd forgotten to care. I didn't ask. And given the Irish tendency toward music, conversation, and storytelling as art rather than scribbling-down-on-paper, determining which poet first took that ten-stress rhyming system from the blacksmith shop to the page is impossible. So I'll just say the inventor is Jim McAuley. And anyway, the Story of it matters more than the Who. Think about it, we can trace a lot of things precisely to their source, and then yawn. For instance, whoever invented Velcro probably has a load of boring specifics on Wikipedia, but I don't care enough to spend five seconds now and see. I'm much more interested in this question of invention, of *originality*. What does it mean?

Take me: I'm a writer, I'm originally from the Northwest, and I'm imprinted by place. So it's possible I've written things that were already "said" a thousand years ago in the carving of a totem pole, and it's possible those things were said a hundred years before that—by the wind, back when the future totem pole was still a sapling.

And where did the wind first hear those phrases? And where did that wind originate?

For another $200.00, you can phone me your guesses, but the answer is Washington or Ireland. Two fine places for stories, and the twins of green.

DOWNHILL SWITCHBACKS AHEAD

To anyone outside of Washington, my hometown is unpronounceable: Puyallup. Heck, I even hear outsiders mispronounce Spokane (sounds like *can* not *cane*), so good luck with my town, stranger.

But I actually lived outside the city limits, in Pierce County, so to make it easier I'll just say I grew up on South Hill and then tell you about two ways we used to get down. One was Woodland Avenue, a straight shot down to Pioneer Way in this mile-long, forty-degree angle. The other was 128th, I think, but that far out—to the cliff edge over the Orting Valley—who really knows? The roads out there were more of a memory map than a system of signs with street names, and unlike Woodland the road to the Orting Highway was more like a snake's dream of dancing. It wound through the trees, so no sightlines. And no streetlights. And one time no headlights either since the car I drove was an antique T-Bird with corroded dust for wiring; the lights just cut out at random. Wicked scary. My point is I loved those downhill turns, even while suddenly blind, so writing sonnets was probably inevitable.

Sonnets? Yes, sonnets. Yes, those poems with all the quizable rules. Don't worry, though, I'm not going to drill you, and the rule I like best is the simple one anyway: *Somewhere between the middle and the end, you have to turn.*

In "Win $300.00," I brought up iambic pentameter, so hopefully talking about sonnets now makes sense. I've actually written gobs of them, though I hadn't imagined writing any beyond the one we were all assigned in high school, and I think it's got something to do with that road I used to love to drive: every line like a cliff edge, and no clear vision of what's coming, then a turn in the middle, then a switchback, then you're there—just across the railroad tracks at the stop-sign-final punctuation, where you look out across the valley at Mt. Rainier. Not bad for fourteen lines, and sometimes worth the trouble. Here's what I mean:

SOME THINGS HAVE ONE MEANING, SOME THINGS DON'T:

"I do," for instance, is conditional;
the truth, it turns out, is political;
and equal means that most have equally less.
But words are like elastic, and unless

you're careful not to stretch too far, they won't
snap back... I know what it is to be in love,
and no one has the right to disapprove
of who I love. They might, but they'd be wrong.
What else? Our lives are loaned to us. Not long.
And not to pile up money. Not for power.
And how we pay that loan back does matter:
with interest, yes—with being interested,
by promising and keeping promises,
by caring more and minding much less instead.

Does it turn? You betcha. There's the word "But," for instance, right there in line four, which is a pretty important word in English since it signals a contrast or foreshadows tension. In this case, though, it isn't really the turn (it's more like a shimmy). The turn comes two lines later, after the words "snap back," and I apologize to anyone for whom that's already obvious (I call out during football games too, even though the refs can't hear me). And there's the rhyming, of course, and the use of meter, and sometimes enjambment past the ends of lines so things don't stack up like fourteen boring dishes, though if that's just a bunch of jabber to you, I understand. The gist is this: Sonnets are like puzzles, and puzzles are cool.

Also, they're similar to argumentative essays, but succinct as a fist. What do I mean? I mean their structure is familiar already, drilled into us by Composition classes and all the essays we had to write in school: Thesis ~ Antithesis ~ Synthesis; or, Sweep right ~ Counter-trap left ~ Play-action pass to the tight end over the middle. Or if chess is more your metaphor, then sonnets are like 64 squares within a square, but just as full of possibility. Plus, the meter and rhyme can amp up the impact, even be memorable, which makes them pretty effective as a way to make a point.

But the thing I like best, as I've mentioned already, is the formal requirement to turn, to swerve, to switchback, yet still wind up in the right place (or a better place) by the end. Here's another sonnet to round this out that hopefully comes close to that:

FAILING AT MATH

I do all my spatial figuring
in football fields. It's easier that way.
The old Packard plant, for instance, in Detroit
is sixty-one football fields, which is a lot,
the biggest abandoned warehouse in the States
with underbrush inside now, a few trees,
even rabbits, and rabbits' bones, and coyotes
adding their new sound to Motown....Let's say
further that I want to know the size
of Crater Lake: twenty-two eighty-eight
football fields times four. That deep, blue eye
in Oregon looks back across the years.
Was it warmer when it used to love the moon,
or always cold like this? It can't remember.

I'D RATHER BE A HAWK

Like me, my friend Jason hates sestinas. Here's what he wrote in a poem of his recently:

> I was at a party where
> someone read a sestina,
> and everyone jumped head-
> first into the bushes
> one floor down, the black
> stocking legs of the women
> waving in the crisp November air.

That cracked me up. I'll take some well-timed humor over thirty-nine lines of repetition any day.

And it's not because I lack the discipline or have a gap in my aesthetic. I could use the form if I wanted to. In fact, I have—just once, and ages ago—in a poem called "Pharaoh's Horse Trainer." He's haunted in his sleep by the same recurring nightmare: all those chariot horses drowning when the parted waters closed behind Moses. And each day he combs the Red Sea shoreline for their bones. For him, I figured, the sestina made sense. But that's it. Most subjects aren't so traumatized and obsessive, so why bolt them to a form that is? I'd rather be a hawk or a tide pool or something; those are forms too.

Still, if you can't shake the feeling that sestinas are expected, that writing one is a measure of your skills, then you might like this. It's a form I invented and kept secret up 'til now, and here are the rules: 1) You don't get thirty-nine lines, just fourteen; 2) yes, you still use iambic pentameter; 3) no, you don't use end rhyme; 4) instead, your end words are recycled in set positions, like so—

> The morning wakes up tired and more <u>gray</u>, [1]
> just lifting the sun out of habit, like winding a <u>watch</u>. [2]
> Why bother? Nothing can get warm in this <u>wind</u>, [3]
> and the haze will go on blocking whatever <u>light</u> [4]
>
> tries reaching here—the stars, the moon, <u>daylight</u>, [4]
> all of it gone. Only the snow's not <u>gray</u>, [1]
> and it will be soon ... grit sifting out of <u>wind</u>, [3]
> snow plows dragging their loads of sand. I've <u>watched</u> [2]
>
> it happen every day this week. I've <u>watched</u> [2]
> and listened to them grind along, orange <u>lights</u> [4]
> spinning a kind of spiral web as they <u>wind</u> [3]
> from block to block. And of course the roads are <u>gray</u>— [1]

—and 5) in the last two lines, you return to the original order

(1, 2, 3, 4) with 1 and 3 placed in the middle of the lines and 2 and 4 at the ends. How cool is that? As cool as a hawk or a tide pool, especially since now you can switch things up and use synonyms in place of repetition:

> favorite non-color [1] of progress and watchbands. [2]
> Meanwhile, the wind [3] keeps yelling that we're not the sun. [4]

That's it. I call it the sestonnet. It has the virtue of being shorter. Fewer guests (and that's what your listeners are) will be working the latches on the exit windows.

Haiku, of course, are shorter still, and they can be nice sometimes, like someone seeing you and smiling. A haiku can be good like *Hello* can be good, or *Good-bye*:

> You've heard sharks don't sleep?
> Your heart should be seven sharks.
> Hunting what? More heart.

WHAT WOULD YOU DO WITH A MINI CANOE?

One day my son up and told me, "Hey, Dad, I know a good job for you."

"Yeah?" I said. "What's that?"

He said, "A writer. You know, like a *real* one."

I didn't mind. Quentin was ten years old, and I knew what he meant. He meant a novelist, someone he'd heard of, someone like Rick Riordan, with minotaurs and lightning thieves and some real money earned from his work.

Poets—at least most of us—don't get paid, and not because we're purists about it. We wouldn't say no to dollars, pesos, euros, even drachmas if those are still spendable. Try it; offer a poet some money sometime, and then clock how many seconds it takes to hear "Yes" and "Wow" and "Thanks" and "You're amazing." Probably one.

I started thinking about this back in January, during the Australian Open—I like Federer—because they kept running this Visit Melbourne TV commercial: a montage of iconic scenery along with a recitation of some ballad stanzas by E.J. Brady. It made me think 1) From now on, every commercial has to be like this; make TV stop it with its idiotic screaming, and 2) Melbourne's got to be raking it in off this ad. And the secret to what makes it good isn't secret; it's just rhyme.

How do I know this? Because sometimes people ask me, "Why don't you use rhyme?"

My answer isn't defensive, but I tell them I use it a lot. And not just in sonnets, in free verse too. Take my poem "What Are Your Skills?"—it rhymes, though maybe it would help if I slowed down and highlighted where:

> Every year [at] Sea School
> we were taught [that] glaciers purr
> and ice /floes/, huge
> be/low/ the surface, were sunning [cats].
> <Call> ours a {failed} education.
> If it makes you feel better,
> <call> our hymns under night skies
> (cracked).
> But for thirteen years
> we {sailed} on bluer water.
> And <all> of us /know/ well
> how to arch our (backs).

Or take this short poem, for instance, so short that the rhymes can't hide, and yet they *almost* do. How come? Because internal rhymes are like those color-changing lizards. And even end rhymes can hang around naked and go unseen if there isn't a metrical pattern nudging us to look:

"[TELL] (US) YOUR FAVORITE TIME OF YEAR"

Not [April]
with [all] that dynamite sugar.
Not Au(gust) either—
too *siesta.*
[I'll] {take}
the flung javelin of [fall], please.
Lock up the {rake} shed.
(Just) watch it arc.

"But what if we like our rhymes naked sometimes? What if, now and then, we want a poem that sounds like we expect it to?"

I say, "I agree." Kids aren't the only ones who respond to rhyme and meter. I'm evidence of that myself. After hearing it half a dozen times, I looked up Brady's "Far and Wide," the poem they'd taken those stanzas from. It's in his book called *Bells and Hobbles* (1911). It's got twelve more stanzas than the two in the commercial. And I was right about poets and money; even Brady made his living from something other than his poetry—first as a clerk, and then as a journalist.

Anyway, I doubt this will get me any airtime in Melbourne, but here goes:

What would you do with a mini canoe?
And where would you keep it when you were through?
Would you shrink yourself down and find a big puddle

and paddle around way out in the middle?
Would you shrink yourself small to the size of a bee
and go to the tide pools at the edge of the sea
where the starfish and crabs will look larger than you?
What would you do with a mini canoe?
You could float in your alphabet soup, and each letter
would be so much bigger and taste so much better,
or float in the bath tub—as wide as the ocean—
and paddle real fast, or row in slow-motion.
These are just some of the things you can do
when you're mini enough for a mini canoe.
But where would you keep it when you were through
and changed back again to your own normal size
with your regular feet, hands, mouth, nose, and eyes?
Maybe you'd put it away in your pocket,
or into a drawer with a keyhole and lock it,
or up by your toothbrush next to the sink,
in the dish on the floor where the cat gets a drink,
or under your pillow so all night you'll dream
of the oceans you've been to, and the puddles, and streams.
A mini canoe can fit anywhere.
There's plenty of room up here, or down there.
But be sure to remember wherever you choose ...
because it's no fun to look for lost mini canoes.

ARCHITECTURE

The newest building on my campus isn't good. The inside design is like an airport terminal, and the elevators are a crapshoot; it's anyone's guess from hour to hour if they'll work. It's been thirteen decades since they built the Eiffel Tower, but I bet its lift goes up and down just fine. What else?—it's been under re-construction since the week after we moved in.

But there is one feature about it I really do like: the windows facing south above the courtyard. There's something accidentally great about the glass, the way it bounces sunlight, so sometimes you'll find this zone where the air is forty degrees warmer. Well, not a zone, a small spot, a thin column, maybe two feet by six feet at most. Think of the transporter room on *Star Trek*, only random and diagonal.

If you're anything like me, you want a whole house made of this glass. Better yet, a geodesic igloo: all those surfaces, and mosaic tilts, the panoramic spaciousness, the sun reflecting in a hundred directions through the late-fall forests of Canada.

Think of the bears there—sun-dazzled grizzlies—delaying their hibernation, spending a few days leaning against the trees, these thousand-year evergreens with trunks as warm as August.

They'd track the sun as the morning circled, searching out the next oasis. And they wouldn't do it by smell, though they've got world-record noses. And they wouldn't be guided by eyesight, though they can see around a river bend and upslope into the future. No, they'd navigate by fur and muscle and joy.

And otters too—they'd hang around swimming, taking turns crisscrossing from the hot to the cold, from cousin-of-ice to cousin-of-jacuzzi in an improvised game of hide-and-seek.

Maybe even wolverines, and lynx, those rare ones, most solitary. They'd follow the rumors of *crowsquawk*, arrive, and find it good: plenty of geese zonked out, and rabbits like stove-warm dumplings.

And you there, standing at the window since everything's a window, the whole house, even the staircase to the loft where you're perfectly naked, looking out at a great blue heron drying its wings in the concentrated sunbeams. Or you're dressed. Or you're holding a coffee mug. It's up to you. You decide on the details.

When you close your eyes, is anyone with you? Do they strike you the same way, like sunlight reflected on the place you're standing? Is your heart awake? Is it a ricochet? What will this magic make you feel like next?

ARCHITECTURE II

I'm not an architect. Not unless you count reading *The Fountainhead* in high school, and you shouldn't.

But poets do build things. Sometimes poorly, sometimes well, and I'm betting you know the difference. I'm betting you've read some poems that feel like waiting at the Department of Motor Vehicles, that crime against both patience and design with its purgatory furniture. Fluorescent lights. Linoleum. Dreary air.

That sucks, and I hear you, but you've also known the opposite: poems that feel like going on a really great date, where the food and smells seem to come from God's own kitchen, and the wine is good (whether red, or white and cold), and you take your time so you can keep on talking, and you never want to have to say good-night.

Or you've found the ones like a coffee shop—local and indie, not corporatized—where the tables might wobble a little, but the coffee's not burned and it doesn't come with sprinkles. Even if it's next to a vacuum store, the place feels somehow tucked away, a well-lit city oasis, with ceilings high enough to welcome in the wind if the doors are left open, and they are. And the music coming from the hidden speakers is exactly what you wanted, even before you knew it, like ESP: Men at Work or The Slackers; Altered Images' "Happy Birthday"; Lick the Tins doing Elvis, turning "Can't Help Falling in Love" to Irish whiskey; Simple Minds, or Talking Heads, or Bird since you can't go wrong with Charlie Parker. It's just what the doctor ordered, plus some chairs and exposed brick walls. You could stay here awhile, have another cup, take it all in.

That's what I'm talking about—poems half poem, half table-in-the-corner. Those are the kind I like trying to build, and maybe you'll think this is one:

WHEN I WENT TO WORK AS A SNOW-GLOBE DESIGNER,

I didn't do it for the usual reasons.
I did it to get some practice in
before building my house at the bottom of the ocean.
Less traffic noise, for one thing,
and I've traded crows for manta rays ...
a million fish like clouds
of colorful rain.
And my yard is a coral reef,
and I never shovel the sidewalk
since the snow just floats suspended in my dome.

You ought to come visit me. We could open some wine
and watch the sharks cruise over ...
then sit together by the fireplace,
impossibly warm.

IN THE BEGINNING WAS THE WORD

Despite the political time we're living in now, we can't let Habit and Lack of Imagination win. Habit thinks, "Brown skin shouldn't have a place here," and Lack of Imagination doesn't ask, "Why not?" Habit takes immigrants' kids away since, after all, it threatened to, and Lack of Imagination doesn't ask, "What then? And isn't that excessive for a misdemeanor?" No, it puts on a tie or a skirt suit and tries to shift the blame. It lies about lying. In other words, it falls back on habit, and around and around.

You're damn right it's a vicious circle.

So what can a poem do about it? Call it out. Talk back. Be the opposite, I guess. Remind us *In the beginning was the Word*, then try to use the best ones. That's what King David was up to, I think, not knowing he'd be quoted for three thousand years. Saint Paul didn't know he'd be a saint and that his letters would last for two millennia. And Walt Whitman? When Whitman spoke to the future, he was speaking to Hope. It wasn't a given that we'd hear him; it was just a belief. All of them: writers.

So what's the best way?

How should I know? You ought to see the tumbleweed scribble I produce just looking for some sort of forward direction. Still, I do believe—if I had to pick some basics—that writing well comes down to these four things:

First, poems should be more than ornamental; they should try to be useful. Others have said it a bit differently—the Utah poet Ken Brewer, for instance, said that poems should "offer a name for something in the shadows of our lives"—but they mean the same thing: Poems have jobs. They use the five senses to get at the essential.

Second, we need new myths, fables, and origin stories. These old forms were magnetic and primal and still are. People might think they've heard them all before, and *yeah yeah, I know*, but they haven't heard ours. To ours, they'll listen. They'll recognize the old form but not the new information, and they'll let themselves be taken up for a minute or two to learn the ending. Here's what I mean:

SOMETIMES IT ISN'T THE SAME OLD STORY

You could understand him misunderstanding,
digging such careful holes with his shovel,
sifting in spoonfuls of birdseed—

an honest mistake.
And you could half-understand how he stubbornly finished,
how he aimed his back at everyone laughing
and patted the dirt down
gently with his hands.
But to greet each day with his watering can,
to go on as if he were a gardener, as if he *believed...*
someone finally stomped all the green in his yard,
and that should've been the end of that.
Certainty feels like a flag when you fly it.
It snaps in the wind
and makes the sound of your own good name,
of your own high opinion. It's the opposite of birds.
And it was birds that he was growing, after all:
cardinals, robins, chickadees, starlings.
His seedlings stood up again,
unfurled their branches,
all of them loaded not with blossoms but with song.
That was the season people re-learned amazement,
followed by the autumn when they re-learned amazement again:
One morning he went 'round his yard on a ladder,
he paid no attention to everyone clapping,
just picked each bird and released it into the sky.

ON MARS AS IT IS IN HEAVEN

The penguin wants to be an astronaut.
She wants to trade her tuxedo for a space suit, sushi
for reconstituting cubes, and navigate the stars
like she navigates the sea.
Try and stop her, try and talk some sense;
you'll see her squeeze her flippers into fists.

It wouldn't be the first time.
She's adapted to circumstance before,
quit flying, for instance, stopped sailing the air
to be a submarine.
Now you're saying a girl can't change her mind?
She's been listening to the radio, heard the news on the BBC—
who's better suited for Mars' arctic climate, her or some man?
You're darn-tootin'.
You can't shut progress in the closet; let her go.
Let her be the first to taste Mars' frozen water,
to blast off with bourbon and an ice pick,
to smoke a cigar on the surface.
Or just brilliantly crash and burn.

Third, it isn't just myths that help us to know the unknowable. Other kinds of poems can do that too. The key is to ground them in concrete details we can care about or argue with. I heard the poet Marvin Bell say once, "I like poems whose ideas have their feet in the dirt." Me too.

And fourth, poems should create a vivid moment. And the secret to doing that is action. Meaning, verbs rather than adjectives; meaning, put most of your adjectives in the interrogation chair and ask, "What do you think you're doing here?" Besides, verbs are more descriptive anyway. They zing, groan, stagger, steam, and zip. Verbs can pogo, while an adjective just has a big happy smile while it jumps.

And that's that—four things for your tool box. Put them together with your guts and heart to build the world a better vision. Writers always have.

ELECTRICAL ENGINEERING

1. There are mornings, as the sun comes up, when the overcast travels the Wasatch Front, moving south to north in a long wide line, like the clouds are almost ranging.
2. Backlit this way—with such stark contrasts—it's so much more than gray. And it reminds you.
3. "Reminds you of what?"
4. "That the clouds aren't just one mass, for starters. And second, where bison come from":
5. Long ago, the bison came from the sky. First, a few clouds drifting away, stopping to graze on the tree tops. Then more and more of them joining, sampling flowers, trying out prairie grass, until finally the First Herd gathered by a

winding snowmelt river.

6. Wolves were already waiting, of course, their howling prayers for new challenges answered,
7. and a prayer they'd never even asked for: a three-day snow. Snow they could glide above weightless while the bison sank to their ice-beards, became bulks, became trudging exhaustion—
8. "Yes, that's true. It's basic science: Mass + Blizzard + Foot Design = A Hell of a Lot More Hunt-able."
9. "And somehow that's about circuitry?"
   "Yes. The bison are the diode."
10. Also lightning. You've got to have lightning. Without spark, the clouds are just a way to move water. Just buckets, assembly-line colleagues. Only functional, no love.
11. No love means no Creation Story.
12. You can roll your eyes all you want to, but you're not smarter than Science. Biology births a frog full of poison so that snakes and monkeys won't eat it, then people come along, invent the Cheeto—
13. "No, Cheetos won't be on the test."
14. I know what I'm talking about. Lightning strikes are memory—sometimes sharp enough to sheer off branches—and rolling clouds are bison, and I've seen a bear,
15. up in Priest Lake, Idaho. It was lying in the middle of the road. A road out of nowhere, it seemed, suddenly there overnight.
16. Logging.
17. Anyway, a road so new that the gravel's still got its tooth shape, and the bear's on his back in the sunlight, digging in his heels. Up/down-up/down-up/down-up/down. Using the road as a backscratcher.
18. That's what I mean about love, about needing it. The bear

is the capacitor. Now you can build yourself a circuit, but before you go:

19. Our brains aren't "hard wired." Never be a person who says that. It's a robot phrase about robots—
20. "No, robots won't be on the test."—
21. It's a whole lot better, I think, and also more scientific, to say we carry clouds inside our skulls, our own bony atmospheres.
22. And our dendrites—let's call them lightning since our thoughts flash out across synaptic gaps.
23. Or don't say flashing, call it traveling. Traveling north along the Wasatch Front.
24. What would happen...I mean, what would people do...if construction crews came and disassembled our homes?
25. Magnetic hammers pulling nails from walls and rooftops. Framing and sheetrock separated, and loaded backward onto trucks. Trucks backing out of our neighborhoods, then backing down the highway, all the way to the mill where these machines—electric miracles—fuse everything together. And those logs then winched onto long beds. And those trucks reversing from the city. And hardhat crews with their gloves on, ready to reattach branches, to stand trees back up along lakeshores, up the slopes of waiting mountains. And then bears—alone, or in pairs, or in groups—moving in.
26. This is your Midterm. And, yes, it's still due Monday: What weather is best for a morning like that—sunny, rainy, or overcast? In 623 words, explain your reasons why.

III.

SEVEN SEEDS

CIVICS LESSONS

What happened isn't always interesting. Not compared to what didn't. For instance, decades ago it was decided that the study of government would be called Civics. Not Principles of Design, or Wisdom Forensics, or What Sort of Citizens Elected This Wizard? Those other names got passed over, and it's too bad because learning about acoustics instead of political noise, or the rightness and function of an arch compared to the Electoral College might have made this a country where the fish aren't so full of mercury.

≈

Twenty-four years ago, I crashed my parents' car. It was dark, almost midnight—even everyone's porch light asleep—and the place my parents had moved was new to me: Fox Island, Washington. Maybe without the fog, or if the roads had been straighter, but they weren't—more like a grandma's cursive—and the fog was thick enough to win some kind of award. Add black ice, the dome light, me reading a list of directions, then a curve into yet another down slope, this one into T-intersection, and I only had a second to wonder *Who put a hill in the middle of the road?* and then *bam*. That's what happened. *The actual.*

≈

But I can't help thinking about the stories that didn't, all the ones less fogged in by facts. Like a next-day story at the salvage yard, a story about the tow-truck driver who'd gotten the call. Maybe he noticed my things—a couple books, a yellow notepad—flung on the floor in front of the passenger seat, so he borrowed some paper, wrote a note, and attached it to the bill—

≈

Dear Driver,

Good news is, since you're reading this, you're alive. Bad news is it's time to shop for a car. Judging from the windshield, you're going to want to wait though—perfect impression of your forehead, and blood sort of spiderwebbing in the cracks. Some of your hair there too, a couple strands of it. Car shopping sucks without a headache thrown in the bargain. Speaking of bargains, these guys here won't be giving you one. What they'll offer you, tops, is two-fifty. That's their impound fee, plus my towing, plus another $50 bucks to buy the deed. Got to have the deed before they part it out. I know a yard that'll maybe go $400.00. I'd've taken your car there in the first place, but the Sheriff said "Tow it to the nearest" etc. Anyway, my number's on the bill if you want to call. From your books, I see you're a Lutheran. Pacific Lutheran University Library. I don't still go to Mass much but keep a rosary hanging from my rear-view mirror. Said an "Our Father" for you last night and hope that you're o.k. On a more practical note—and believe me, you're going to want to do this—get all that broken glass in your head out now. Every single sliver. If there's pieces of glass still in there, well, when they start to work their way to the surface you'll have to slice the scars open with an X-acto knife and tweezer around in the infection. Here's the part where I tell you "Wear a seatbelt" like I'm some kind of too-late Guardian Angel. Sincerely, James "Mac" McIntyre. P.S.: I hope you don't think that the Lutheran stuff was me being a jackass criticizing. Just thought you might like knowing about the prayer.

≈

That's what I mean about what didn't happen. What could have is the better, more necessary story.

≈

And here's a third example, this one straight from *The Salt Lake Tribune* (A6, 3 March 2016). What Happened: This senator, Todd Weiler, Republican of Woods Cross, got ticked about members of the Navajo Nation seeking to re-name Columbus Day. During debate on their petition—standing on the floor of the Senate—he said, "The native population gave the early explorers syphilis, which they brought back to Europe. Blaming Columbus for the extermination of the native population is as fair as blaming the native population for people who die using tobacco and cocaine, which the natives introduced to the Europeans."

≈

What Didn't Happen: He wasn't wearing a Pharaoh outfit. Frogs didn't rain from the Senate ceiling. No one had to hopscotch over bright green insights to take a seat, vote *No*, and kill their bill.

MODERN LEGACIES

I teach a Modern Legacies course at Utah Valley University. I call it "Futuristic Fiction: Paranoia or Prophecy?" I supplement novels with stories and film clips, pair them with Plato's *The Republic* and current events. Tolkien's *The Two Towers* isn't part of it. Wrong genre, for starters: too many elves. But *damn* if the Golden Hall of Meduseld isn't a lot like Pennsylvania Avenue, and isn't the motive of Wormtongue exactly the same?—unchecked self-promotion. Think of what Tolkien's creep could have done with a gizmo as wormy as Twitter.

≈

Worse, our Wormtongue-in-Chief has Wormtongues of own—*whisper whisper*—like Ryan Zinke suggesting, for instance, that too much land and ocean life are being preserved. "My ass!" roars Teddy Roosevelt. He wads up Zinke's monuments report, yells, "Pull," and blasts it from the air. "Good shot, Mr. President." "I don't need flattery from suck-ups, Junior." Then the spirit of Roosevelt exits. End of scene... How beautiful would that be? The sun taking a last look back before setting, turning the Potomac River to silver, and Zinke alone with his thoughts, whatever they are. I doubt they'd be this: *We ought to make the Grand Canyon smaller.* But I don't know for sure.

≈

Here's something you might not know: Back in the days of its designation, locals opposed the Grand Canyon. "Strictly mineral country," they called it. This was when it was all just flatland, see? So they dug, and picked, and shoveled after treasure. They hoisted with pulleys. Their pack mules hauled rock. But the only thing they uncovered was a river, and eons of useless view.

≈

It's time now to mention Montana: Stepping down from the bus in Polson, nothing but an orchard between me and Flathead Lake. It looked like the Rockies were floating on the water. There's a word for that. It's *reflection*...Or that spot along the Clark Fork River where the piling is topped by an osprey nest ... Or rounding a hilltop highway, bound for Great Falls, and openness everywhere, suddenly there, forever as the ocean, only green, all grass and no billboards, and the road straight out in front of me up to the sky. Well, not really; that was just the feeling: so much, and so all-at-once, that I had to stop the truck. It was making my eyes tear.

≈

Secretary Zinke, you're from there, so what's going on? What's wrong with your vision? Are the tribes of Utah—past, present, future—worth less than others in your factoring? Imagine right now that I'm your teacher, and it's fourth-grade math; I'm saying, "Show me your work." And imagine, further, that you're listening. Not tuned-out-staring, but for real: Pacific tuna will never recover, not if you "right size" Maritime Monuments, and "The Creator of All" means Creator of atolls, of coral, of moray eels. Or imagine that Karma is a shark, and you're boatless, probably dead from thirst and exposure, which is maybe merciful and maybe not, depending on your view of the oceanic whitetip.

≈

If you soaked the moon in napalm, lit it on fire, that's Northern Canada. That's the trading of tar sands for land and air, immeasurable in miles per gallon.

≈

Sometimes I wonder what the future will think, assuming that people are a part of it. How many RPMs on their constant question: *Why?*

SEVEN SEEDS

Some things, even important things, like another news day of scandal—the whole ditch-flow of murk where there ought to be a president—flow by, and you don't hear them. But throw a rock—throw ninety—in a river, and you listen every time: that splash, that *splunk*, that ricochet-click off a boulder, the pa-*lop* from a bigger rock lofted where it's deeper...every time...and four crows *scrawking*; I guess they like it too. This could be any river. It doesn't have to be the Cowlitz. You don't have to be a kid like I was, spending the weekend with my friend's family at their cabin: an A-frame somewhere called Packwood, close to White Pass. I went to sleep wondering, would your thoughts be different if you lived by a river? Colder, maybe? Always moving? Knowing the way?

≈

Of course, this happened a long time ago. There might have been three crows, or five, not four. They were blacker than the ones on the playground at our school. There were boulders in the river stacked with snowcaps. And the sky seemed grayer, like the clouds were lower, but they weren't. We were just in the mountains.

≈

Maybe what's needed is a flipbook so the president can understand, can flip ahead to see the outcome in advance: Pick Betsy DeVos for Education—*flip*—and see it gone, defunded, thrown away; or pick Scott Pruitt, make him EPA Director—*flip*—and now we're in Alaska by a poisoned Bristol Bay. Who knew? Who could have predicted?—that a gold mine called Northern Dynasty Minerals would ever cause harm, would toxify a watershed, would fill up streams with chemicals, would starve the tribal nations and force them to move? Sixty million salmon knew. And four thousand acres of tundra. And an earthquake zone. And a flipbook. Everyone knew. Well, maybe not Wayne LaPierre. He's pretty single-minded. Here's Wayne LaPierre as Marie Antoinette: "Let them eat machine guns."

≈

I know a man named Lee Boulet. I've known him my whole life. He's the opposite. When he goes to the mountains in the fall, he fills his truck with a load of pumpkins. Elk step out from the trees when he gets there. Like solid ghosts. Like antlered thankfulness. They stand around eating for an hour, rinds and stems and all... The Boulet's back yard slopes down to Clark's Creek, and one time Lee was in his waders, fishing. In books, fish lived in the ocean, so this wasn't right, wasn't true; I was a kid; I thought he was teasing me, but no. Salmon would swim right by sometimes, back to spawn, probably near the hatchery. First-graders went there on field trips, so I should have known: thousands of fingerlings released in Clark's Creek ~ the Puyallup River ~ Commencement Bay ~ Puget Sound ~ the Strait of Juan de Fuca ~ then the open ocean ~ then back again. It's quite a journey. Even without all the concrete dams. Even without a kid on the bank with a net.

≈

The dams are a problem, so people try solutions, some of them simple as a fish ladder, some of them not. I like the one with the vacuum system, and a tube like a giant straw. Salmon get drawn from the base of the dam, water and all—sucked up and pumped over. What a weird story to pass on as archetype, imprint on the next generation: *Then you shall come to the Place of Reversal, where the river suddenly pulls, and you rise and you're launched into flying, but do not fear.* Another way isn't so magical. They're just driven around in trucks: into the bed, up the road, then dumped back out, which sounds boring 'til you think about it; who *does* that job, and what is their title? Ichthyological taxi driver, endangered-salmon chauffer, the perfect gig for a Pisces, the catcher in the rye?...well, not rye but the river. Someone with Salinger's book on the dashboard, reading a bit between runs, and Holden calling out the phonies for doing this to fish, to water, to the ocean's pulse: *goddamn.*

≈

There's this dove outside now, picking up twigs and the bleached leaves of last year's irises. He's setting them down again, picking them up. He's not acting on impulse; he's weighing. Then he flies to my roof, then somewhere else, then back for more. He's building a nest. He's putting his beak to good use, a real purpose, while the president can't use his own mouth for anything but lies and slurs and a stream of idiot-splutter. "You know, I really believe," he said, "you don't know this until you test it ... but I think I ... I really believe I'd run in there even if I didn't have a weapon." This about a high school massacre, seventeen murdered in Florida. And then this about teachers bringing guns to work, another thing for their supply lists: whiteboard markers, and a three-hole punch, and construction paper, and an EpiPen, and the number for Family Services, and patience as long as river, and now also guns: "I want highly trained people," he says, "that have a natural talent. Like hitting a baseball, or hitting a golf ball, or putting. How come some people always make the four-footer?" I don't know. But that's not the question. The question is, what sort of bird would build a nest with that?

≈

The dove's been at it all day; that's one thing. And my cat's been patient; that's another. He knows that sometimes birds forget he's there, stray close and get lazy. He can move like a river when he wants to, *swift*, a cascade over his foreclaws, then a heavy stillness like water piled behind a log fallen down across the current. This could be any river. It doesn't have to be the Cowlitz—like the Methow in the Okanogans, flowing past Twisp; or the Pearl; or the Green in central Utah; you can fill in whatever name you want; that's what water would do. But don't forget this: By now some seeds have taken root up there, hidden in the Cascade Mountains, all those evergreens and ferns now dotted with orange: a patch of pumpkins. I can copy my map for you, that way we'll have a secret. Our own good thing that keeps growing, where we can go back.

TRAVELING THROUGH TIME

There's a road sign along I-70 near the Utah/Colorado border that says, "Travel Through Time." I didn't exit, though. I figured it wasn't being literal, just giving directions to a byway through eons of rock, these cool striations layered like chapters in *The Book of This Planet*, yes, but I wouldn't actually be exiting 2019.

≈

I was driving back from a reading I'd done in Ridgway, Colorado—The Open Bard Series—and everyone was nice, a whole townful of Arts District patrons; you should go. Early March. They call it "Mud Season" there, like it's spring's first flower or crop, like this town is the spot mud aims for in its annual migration, herding in or winging down then getting busy with some serious breeding: mud displays to spark female attention, mud challengers to last year's champion, mud anthems and warbles and bugle calls—they named it right. The yards and streets were muddy.

≈

Since I grew up in western Washington, the capital of rain, I know about mud. We used to play football in it, our town's two high schools having to share one field at the old Sparks Stadium. The grass didn't last. How could it? It never got a Friday night off, so by mid-October, things were a slogfest of mud, mud that smelled like crab shells and fish rot, like an act of penance, almost holy. The grounds crew figured adding sand was a good idea—*Maybe dry things out a bit. Maybe solid-up the footing a little*—but they were wrong. Now there was grit on top of all the rest. Grit in your mouthpiece. Grit between your forehead and helmet pads rubbing ... we'd hit the showers with our uniforms still on, all our pads and cleats and everything. Layers of sediment, win or lose, washing away.

≈

Nobody younger than me has a story like that. They burned down the stadium. Simple enough to do since they'd built it with wood. Our yearbook included a photo of it: flame-waves crashing into fire-cliffs, and more flame spraying up. It really hit me, I don't know why ... The new stadium has Astroturf, and they crowned it in the middle for drainage, and the only smells now are normal ones: sweat and popcorn, maybe perfume from the marching band girls.

≈

Maybe I just like old things. My coat, for example; it's old. It gets compliments: the guy at Hruska's making morning food, Jenny McDonald at her Mardi Gras party, people walking by me on campus—they say, "I like your coat." I've had it for thirty-one years. It's forty years older than that. I found it in a thrift store near Tacoma in 1988. And my clocks: an old pendulum one from a second-hand store in Spokane, and another that used to hang in my grandparents' house: from the 1950s, wood and metal, this atomic-looking sun. And my antique furniture, my standing lamps and old cabinets ... I guess it's like that sign in Colorado: traveling through time.

≈

It might be one of those weird things while driving, when it's hours of your own thoughts and not much else, but the Colorado Plateau buttes and mesas seem to move, to float along west-northwest, a barnacled armada. This isn't the ocean; I know that. And the smoke rising up from those mesas is only clouds. That's the sky; it's only overcast; but still ... Maybe all the sagebrush dotted around could be bison if they'd just stand up, if they'd just quit kneeling and stampede, or graze, or walk on over here and hijack the freeway. If it took all day for them to cross, I wouldn't mind. I could wait for that miracle.

≈

Here's what I mean about patrons: The people of Ridgway have filled their town with poems. They're painted on metal and bolted to walls. There's a map; you can tour them and read, like walking around in a book, a book with a binding of sky and trees and a cat stretched out in a windowsill lit up with sun. We could use a lot more of this. Town after town. A whole library.

≈

MUD VS. NOT-MUD: A bucket of clams is mud, but kidnapping refugee children while you're lying through a policy smile: not mud at all; there's mud and there's slime, and there's a difference, and if the Secretary of Homeland Security doesn't know that, something's wrong and crucial things are broken inside her... My bad-ass Maine Coon cat, he's mud. He's got a new way of going outside: stalking in a circle 'round the chair while I open the door, then a *lunge-dash* past me out to the porch. What is he practicing? I don't know, but I know it's mud. And Robert Frost is mud, and "Harrison Bergeron" by Vonnegut, but the novels of Thomas Hardy (I'm sorry) aren't mud, at least not to me. Making the coffee with a French press: mud. The Utah Utes in the Rose Bowl: mud. And that band from the Northwest, Modest Mouse, "Float On": like mud that's learned to sing.

IV.

RACCOON VERSES

SPELLING

I was a spelling tutor once for three Arab guys—Mohammed, Muhammed, and Khalid. We'd meet and I'd agree that it's a pitchfork curse, that *zoo*, *blue*, *shoe*, *through*, *view* and *two* shouldn't rhyme; that *heart* with *part*, and *haunt* with *want*, and *reign* with *brain* were insane—and then we'd go shoot pool.

Muhammed was the best at it, an extrovert, always smiling, so on the day he said he didn't want to, I could tell that he was feeling down.

"I miss camels," he said. "Here there are only cows."

To hell with idioms. He'd hit on a better way to say, "I'm homesick." And right now, sitting in my house, I'm homesick too. Not for camels, for water.

Astrology tells me there's a reason for this. My zodiac sign is the Crab, and I'm landlocked. Four-thousand feet above sea level. Utah.

But just like with spelling—an *e* on the end makes the vowel sound long, but not in the case of the number "one"—there must be exceptions. I mean, somewhere there's bound to be a Taurus (Earth sign) who totally lives to water ski, or a Virgo (another Earth sign) who up and buys a kayak in her thirties, turns herself halfway into an otter, even inventing new coves in her sleep, and new woods with accessible places to launch from. One night she finds her arms moving under the blankets, enough that she wakes herself up: It's the middle of the night, it's her bedroom, and the nearly fluid sunlight cutting through the overcast was just a dream. The sound of her paddle dipping, dipping, dipping in the lake was just rain outside getting scooped at her house by wind gusts. The weather and her limbs tuned and rhythmic. Liquid whispers.

Water: Mix it with grain and time, you get whiskey; with pigment and talent, you get art; with salt, and now you have a home for orcas. Mix it with imagining and memory, and I don't feel quite so homesick anymore.

How do you spell "kayaker"? W-a-t-e-r.

How do you spell "hypnotic"? W-a-t-e-r.

How do you spell "want" and "heart" and "rain"? W-a-t-e-r.

MAYBE NOT EDEN, BUT SOME KIND OF GARDEN

Am I the only one who thinks about Medieval Drama?

Probably.

But it isn't boring, especially not that cardiac interlude: The Parade of the Seven Deadly Sins. This was everyone's favorite part, the reason they came out and endured all the moralizing weather. They came to see the Sins storm in and barge through the middle of the allegory, to see the actors in personified costumes thieve and belch. They liked the raging, the strutting, the feathery lust. And if you think that sounds kind of cool now after all, you're right, which is why we still have plenty of it around today.

What's Mardi Gras, for instance? It's the parade of the seven sins set free from the heard-it-before storyline. It's the jack-in-the-box without the dogma box. It's jazz without the dirge.

And it isn't alone. Remember *The Breakfast Club*? The dancing scene in the library is an '80s approximation of the Parade of the Seven Deadlies set to Karla DeVito singing "We Are Not Alone."

Or more recently (and so brilliant), there's *The Brothers Bloom*, specifically the scene in the middle where Bloom is on his own: no dialogue, no plot advancement, just idling the day away in Prague while the audience hears "Miles From Nowhere" by Cat Stevens. What a song. Anyway, Bloom gets this impulse to pocket an apple—the single red one on a stack of greens—only the vendor's kid spies it, and Bloom gives him a look like *Maybe we can keep this between us. Please*, but the kid points at Bloom and yells to his father, and here we go: Bloom is off and running, high-step-flying down the hillside, joy on his face, ecstatic, totally thrilled. He's the rhythm and melody of the soundtrack embodied, and suddenly *Wham!* he trips, and we jump cut edit to his older brother bailing him out of jail:

STEPHEN: An apple?

BLOOM: Yeah. It was part of an epiphany.

Then they hug, exit, and the song resumes, and holy crap it's awesome. Bring on more carnival detours like that one.

Of course the most famous of these instances is in *Butch Cassidy and the Sundance Kid*. Yes, the bicycle scene: Newman and Katherine Ross. Unforgettable. Who doesn't want to learn to do those bicycle tricks? Who's shaken out of historical context by that Burt Bacharach tune? I know the song's wrong for the early 1900s. Heck, it was wrong for 1969, the year the film was released; London had Led Zeppelin, screaming and guitaring; San Francisco had Janis Joplin with Big Brother and the Holding Company scorching the posters off the walls of the Fillmore West; so what's going on with "Raindrops Keep Falling on My Head"? I don't know, but it works.

There's just something about these interludes. There always has been. We need more than forward progression; ask a river. And while you're standing there on the riverbank, start looking for a rock to skip. If there's wind, let yourself notice. What does it smell like? It smells like *cold*. Listen to the crunch of leaves if you want to. If something or someone makes you curious, then go ahead and wonder. This isn't sloth, and it isn't deadly.

Let your senses attend the parade.

LINGUISTICS

Salt Lake City:

I made a quick stop at *7-11* this morning to grab what, a Kind Bar? a Power Bar?—oh, marketing, you're so ridiculous—and a second cup of coffee, and at the register I said, "This is a re-fill," and the clerk said, "Use the app, honey, so it's free," and I said, "I don't have a phone," and she said sorry and rang me up the extra buck-fourteen. Not sorry that I don't own a cell phone; it was way too early to get existential. She meant she wished that she didn't have to charge me.

I didn't mind paying, but there are two things now that I'm wondering: First, do people really put up with spam and corporate tracking in exchange for a cup of coffee? And second, would my kid look over my shoulder at this and tell me, "That's a lot of *ands* in that paragraph, Dad"? His teacher, I guess, has a rule against it.

The problem isn't all the ands, though. It's the word "app," which isn't actually a word so much as a tone-deaf, lame abbreviation. And it isn't alone. It's got company—"twitter," "tweet," and "hashtag," for instance. Linguists would call them neologisms, but they're the worst, "hashtag" especially. "Hashtag" is the rake you step on so your face gets cartoon handle-smacked. Ever try *uni* (raw sea urchin)? That stuff is hashtag. It tastes like the tide flats, can't be swallowed, doesn't chew. It just amoebas around in your mouth and won't go down, like a dog-slobbered racquetball. It's got to be the dumbest word ever, and there isn't an app to get rid of it. No, our only recourse is to stay on the side of aesthetics and memory, and since this all started with coffee, here are two memories about that—the first one set in Spokane and the other one in Ireland.

Spokane:

The all-at-once-everywhere espresso bug originated in Seattle, but it didn't take long before it spread across the state. It crossed a mountain range, range lands, the Columbia River, miles and miles of wheat fields, and *shazam!*—cappuccino kiosks appearing overnight, one of them a hundred yards from where I lived (South 608 Stevens, the Altadena Apartments, just down the hill from St. John's Cathedral). Two young women were running it, both of them mythically beautiful. I unplugged and shoved aside my coffee maker. It seemed like the right thing to do.

But it didn't last. Each double latte cost more than a pint, and I could do the math. Pretty baristas have their upside, but beer is beer.

Ireland:

A year later, mid-summer, I was billeted in Dublin. That's their word for it, "billeted"; meaning, something less than a boarder but more than passing through. Anyway, each night our host asked us (my friend Tod was there too; we were students), "What would you like for breakfast tomorrow?" and I'd say, "Coffee, please, if you have it," and each morning she'd bring out eggs, blood pudding, pots of tea. Good tea. Tea I could really get used to. In fact, I even got insistent about it one weekend out in Sligo. Tod and I had gone there for a music festival, and maybe to check out Inisfree, but first—this was Tod's idea—we needed to climb Queen Mab's burial mound.

It wasn't even 6 a.m., so I said no. Wouldn't you? I didn't want to hike for miles, climb a hill, then climb the mound itself, which wasn't nothing...more like another hill stacked on top of the first one. Forget it. Not until I've had some cups of tea.

Did I mention we were loud? That most of Europe was still sleeping?

Well, this man must have been an early riser himself, and must have heard our American racket, because as we passed his door he was standing there, waiting to invite us in. Tea: He was on my side about it.

He set his kettle on a hot plate, spitted some bread on a bent wire hanger, waved it slowly over the gas-range flames, and there was toast. Extremely nice.

Here and Now:

As for aesthetics, that's easy. Pick any good poem, and you're bound to find some. E.E. Cummings, for instance, gave us "mudluscious" and "puddlewonderful" for spring. Or there's Milton. This one's from *Paradise Lost*. When he needed a word that didn't exist yet, some way to make hell seem real on the page, he grabbed a prefix, a root, and a suffix and came up with "pandemonium." In "Vulture," Robinson Jeffers called the soul's ascension "enskyment." Of course. What else could the afterlife be when joined with those telescope eyes and that living wingspan?

And don't forget Anne Sexton. She's an alchemist. Start with "Hurry Up, Please, It's Time," especially the part where she's out in her backyard, celebrationally naked, saying, "Sun, you hammer of yellow, / you hat on fire, / you honeysuckle mama, / pour your blonde on me!" Absolutely. Though that does stretch things a bit since those aren't neologisms. Technically, they're epithets, but I *really* like hearing them: phrases she lines up like shots of tequila.

They're so much better than "Hit me on twitter," "Send your tweets to #hashtag whatever," and "Be sure to download the Free Coffee App @whyamIdoingthis.com."

DOWN HERE ON THE COLD, COLD GROUND

With the New Year not so long ago, and in the spirit of resolutions, I plan to spend a minute each morning hating the guts of Vlad Sitnikov. He's the project leader of this startup called StartRocket, and what he wants to do by 2020 is steal the night for himself and sell it for ad space.

This is true. A student at Utah Valley University (UVU) named Elijah Williams sent me a note with a link to an article in something called *Futurism*. When I read it, I figured it was satire, like *The Onion*. Either that, or a hoax. Not according to Media Bias/Fact Check, though; I checked. *Futurism* is legit. So that means Vlad Sitnikov is real, and his words and rationalizations for sending up cube satellites to glow logos at all of us from space are real too. There's even a little *vimeo* to give us the idea: a logo in the way of the Aurora Borealis; another floating over Paris (the City of Lights, for God's sake); and that crappy KFC lettering in front of the stars above the Utah desert, over places like Capitol Reef that have been designated International Dark Sky Parks... Anyway, Vlad Sitnikov. You should hate him too.

About why he ought to get away with this, and with charging whichever corporations whatever gobs they'll pay, he said, "We are ruled by brands and events." He said, "The economy is the blood system of society. Entertainment and advertising are at its heart." All of which is wrong. I don't just mean unethical and empty; I mean incorrect.

People are the heart of society. We might put up with ads, or become numb to them, or get influenced or not, but if ads are the heart of society, then no amount of Peloton sweat and Geico harassment and Arby's creepiness and Verizon flunkies can ever defibrillate society back to life. "Corpsed" is all that is. "Corpsed": I'm borrowing the expression from Beckett's *Endgame*, a play about nihilism so brilliantly put together that you can't help feeling more alive, somehow affirmed, because there are people so good at making things—existential plays, books, dinners, lesson plans, fast-break alley-oops off the dribble, music (I'm looking at you, Tom Waits), chess moves, well-timed funny remarks—people so good at making things that you're glad you're alive just to notice them.

And people are the blood system too. The economy could be anything—goats, rum, seashells—and has been. So the hell what? I'd rather have transactions of kindness. I'd rather bank on ethics, education, creativity. I'll value the purring of cats, and the possibility of seeing a mountain lion, and the way it smells in summer after it rains: almost new, but also dusty. I'll take all of those, plus memories, and the taste of just-picked peaches. They seem a lot more like lifeblood, at least to me. I mean, if the Renaissance were just a period of mercantile capitalism without literacy, cathedrals, and art, then who would care?

As for being "ruled by brands and events," I don't know what Sitnikov's talking about, although admittedly reading "This Startup Wants to Launch Giant Glowing Ads Into the Night Sky" (Jon Christian, *Futurism*, 8 Jan. 2019) has kept me busy writing this for hours. I guess you could say getting Elijah's email was an "event."

But here's the bigger story: It's been a few semesters since Elijah took my class, an Honors course called Modern Legacies. Our focus was "Futuristic Fiction: Paranoia or Prophecy?" As part of it, I asked students to bring in or email articles that seemed relevant to the ideas and warnings in works by Bradbury, Orwell, Wells, and Huxley, etc.—things they found that were interesting enough to share with me and with each other. Disturbing things, or heartening things, either way. The point was to connect our present time to either 1) dystopias, or 2) better alternatives with less pollution, less economic haves vs. have-nots, smarter food and energy production, smarter conservation and transportation, less T&A-driven shallowness, more wildness and wild animals, less veering toward demagogues and oligarchies, and all of them did. And some, like Elijah, have kept on doing it. Not because they're "ruled" but because they're interested. Sitnikov might call that the UVU "brand," but not me. To me the language of business is like stepping in gum.

Not that there aren't brands I like. I do. I like Häagen-Dazs. I buy Community Coffee. I get all my shoes from Fluevog's. If somebody asked, "You want a Foster's?" I'd say yes and drink that beer. Maybe there'd be a stereo too. And a stack of CDs to look through. Maybe Camper Van Beethoven's *Key Lime Pie*.

And then Tom Waits singing "Cold Cold Ground."

MUSIC HISTORY

The first time I heard The Grateful Dead was on KOMO AM 1000, and I was hooked at age 9. It's an improbable origin story since KOMO was usually the source of Sonics basketball games, news, and Paul Harvey, but it's true.

More recently—today, in fact—The Dead were on satellite radio, a whole channel just for them. Am I the only one who didn't know this already? It's not the same as CDs, but it's still pretty great.

What I like about The Dead isn't esoteric or anything. It's pretty plain. When you hear them, it sounds like they're just taking their instruments out for a walk. There's a breeze but no serious wind, nothing that smacks of effort, just the sun and clouds working out the temperature together the way a kid works out which stick to float in the river next. What I mean is, they show us that music doesn't have to feel *worked on* to be *arrived at.*

And that's true of movies too. Take *Jaws* and *Jurassic Park*, for instance. Obviously the animatronic T-Rex and raptors look more believable than the shark. It probably helps that the dinosaurs' electronics didn't have to work while submerged in the water. But the bigger point is that *Jurassic Park*, despite its advantage in mechanics, feels so made, so much like a movie, and *Jaws* doesn't, at least not to me. *Jaws* feels like we're there ourselves on Amity Island, or swimming in the ocean surrounding it, or on the piers in the harbor, or slopping chum from a bucket while we're rockingly seasick and breathing diesel fumes straight from the Orca's squeezebox engine. We're the people Quint keeps laughing at and then singing "You Fair Spanish Ladies." We're in the dining room with Hooper at the Brodys' house. We're the overwhelmed deputy holding up a hand-painted sign while the scene on the street is a crowd of greedy bozos blitzing the shelves in the bait shop. Nothing—and especially not when Quint recounts the story of the U.S.S. Indianapolis—feels manufactured or difficult, though according to Spielberg, Scheider, Dreyfuss, and others—I've seen interviews—it was an ocean-sized strain of a movie to make. And I believe them. But it sure is easy to watch.

Same thing with teachers, and I've been lucky enough to have some good ones: Jim Taylor (Rogers High School) and Tom Campbell (Pacific Lutheran University, the PLU Lutes; short for Lutherans, though also that In-the-Beginning instrument given to us by Hermes when he scooped out a turtle, added frets and strings, and invented the bardic tradition).

What Mr. Taylor did was teach A.P. English to teenagers, somehow revving us up about *Heart of Darkness*, and J. Alfred Prufrock, and writing character analyses, all without appearing to "teach." He didn't treat literature like a can you pry open then dump out the can-shaped answers, and he didn't act scripted. No, it was more like Wallace Stevens' line in his most anthologized poem: "Let be be finale of seem." Mr. Taylor never had to *seem to* because he was *being it*.

And Professor Campbell was the same. How he taught Advanced Composition through the thunder-noise of McChord Air Force Base—it's practically next door to campus—I don't know, but he did it. Not easy, not easy at all, though he made it look that way.

I like poems that pull off this same kind of magic: Built Things that Seem as Unconstructed as a Forest.

Take Anne Sexton; wow, can she do this. In "The Ambition Bird," to pick just one example, she hoists the Sistine Chapel, sends the Magi out on stage, yet still makes drinking cocoa the real stakes in her poem. "That warm brown mama," she calls it.

Or take Richard Garcia, his poem "The Story of Keys." It's like The Grateful Dead meets origin story, meets the bow-legged grace of Charlie Chaplin, meets red wine. It's fantastic top to bottom, and then he ends it this way: "Anything can be a key: a piece of wire, / a safety pin, laughter."

It's perfect as is, I know, but to Garcia's list of anythings I'm going to add a lute. Hermes used his to entertain Zeus and con Apollo, and he did all this, if I remember correctly, on the day that he was born, which is some pretty genius work without looking like either.

My cat has that skill set, Anne Sexton had it, *Jaws* bit it in half and became it. And The Grateful Dead?—they went ahead and put it to music while seeming surprised that they knew what they were doing: *Oh, oh, and I wa-ant to kno-ow, how does the song go?* That's from "Uncle John's Band," bardic and elemental, a song like a sunlit river trading stories with the wind.

MUSIC HISTORY II

Two things happened that got me thinking.

This was during the Get Lit! Literary Festival, and I was staying at the Red Lion at the Park, standing out back on one of the footbridges, listening to the Spokane River. Airports, hotel lobby, various conventioneers at various conventions, all in that fleecy-vest type of get-up, so maybe you can understand what happened: Out of the corner of my eye I spotted a man walking up, pulling his rolling carry-on luggage. He stops to fidget, and I turn back to watch the river pouring through the open floodgate. Then I catch him again, crossing the bridge behind me, only he doesn't have a suitcase at all. He's walking his dog. He's holding a leash.

Perception is crazy weird. Either the brain takes shortcuts, or it's trickable, or both. So that was the first thing.

The second is I'd gotten an email from my friend Jamie. He's the lead singer in a Steely Dan cover band in Seattle called Nearly Dan—good name—and I'd asked about his recent gigs, and he told me performing is a blast but that he misses the way we used to play music back in college. Meaning, on an actual turntable.

We even had a sort of duel going, one or the other of us leaving a record spinning and a note saying something like "Drop the books, then the tone arm, and get your real education," or "Try to beat this one, dumbass," and it would be a lesser-known track from Joni Mitchell's *Don Juan's Restless Daughters*, or "Dangerous Type" off *Candy-O* for a kick-back four-minute flashback since we'd grown up listening to The Cars. The exact record doesn't matter, and it isn't the point. The point is that cuing up music on the internet isn't the same. Jamie was saying that in his email, and I agree: Pandora.

Pandora is the roller-wheeled suitcase rather than the actual dog. It's misperception. And as a name, it's pretty lame and upside down because whoever made it up was skipping the facts: Pandora's Box wasn't a good thing, not unless you want blight to fly out and everything nice to be lost except for hope. Tactile connection?—gone. Design and aesthetics?—*whoosh.* Intention, progress, and resolution?—voided out in favor of disconnected singles, then some others like synonyms, and so on. She shouldn't have her name misused that way, especially not after the mythological whammy the Ancient Greeks gave her in the first place, the same bad rap as Eve: "Don't open that box, and don't touch that fruit tree. Just sit there and die of curiosity." Followed by: "Well, thanks to you two, everyone's going to have allergies now. And zits and mucous and cancer. They'll all stink, and struggle, and women will yell their guts out in childbirth, and people will be cursed with mosquitos and TV commercials and then robbed of their autonomy in old age. All because of you." That's a suck-ass story if you think about it, but I'll still take the original Tragedy over today's new Whatever-You-Call-It, with software doing your choosing for you based on stuff you already know you like. Maybe if it sparked curiosity, or if Spotify did, or the next thing comin' 'round the mountain, but nope; they just replace our curiosity with I-Don't-Know.

Q: What's in the box?

A: Just more boxes.

Q: Can I have a bite of your apple?

A: If I can have a bite of yours.

There used to be whole albums, these constructed sonic worlds, arranged in order and jacketed with cover art and liner notes. And sometimes those liner notes were like anthropological essays, or like eulogies for gone-away eras. Check out The Violent Femmes, for example: *Add It Up (1981-1993)*. Or Nat Hentoff and others on jazz recordings. Reading the liner notes on Charles Mingus' *Mingus Ah Um* (Columbia 1959) is how I was reminded about what an opportunistic, race-baiting creep Governor Orval Faubus was. If his name's not familiar, you can Wiki him, but I'd rather have "Fables of Faubus" spinning while I read from a record jacket I can hold in my hands. If I have to remember Faubus at all, or notice similarities between him and politicos these days ("Pandora, find me a present-day Orval-Eugene-type; bingo, out pops somebody yelling about Mexicans, Muslims, and women who aren't in his beauty pageants), then doing it via keystrokes or swiping would only make it worse.

But getting back to music—I bet you could tell Siri to sing Duran Duran's "Hungry Like The Wolf" and get something that sounds like an existentially sad Chihuahua. Or say, "Alexa, play 'Ring Them Bells' by Bob Dylan," and no doubt the song will play. But even so—even if you're sitting by someone amazing, someone who's never heard this song before—it isn't the same as lowering the tone arm, or opening the CD case and then the tray ...

From that place on the footbridge over the Spokane River, you can see the dam, the open floodgates, colossal water pouring through and climbing the concrete banks of the channel, and it's pretty cool. But it isn't my favorite spot. The river is the least itself there and more like *somebody else's*. It isn't a whole album, just a packaged single. On repeat,

repeat,

repeat,

repeat,

repeat.

TWO CURES FOR BILLBOARDS

In the Blue Mountains up in Oregon, they don't mess around. It's different than eastern Washington, where I thought I'd seen a sign for Ultimatum Ridge. Only I didn't. It was one of those eye-skip things. Southbound on I-82, winding into Yakima County, what you really see is a sign for Umtanum Ridge. Which is fine, of course, and not nearly as lightweight as my own state of Utah—Sandy, Park City, Pleasant Grove, and a town, no kidding, called Bountiful. Not so in the Blues. True, there's LaGrande (rhymes with "the hand"), but before you twist down through the mountains to get there, you'll pass signs along the freeway for Deadman Pass, Poverty Flat Road, Old Emigrant Hill

Road, even something called Steer's Bones. A gulch, canyon, avalanche dance club? I don't know, but it sure isn't Bountiful.

Even better, there are signs that say, "Max Fine for Littering $6,520." Holy cow. *Holy steer's bones!* And now I want to do that in Utah too, and also redefine "litter," since to me the biggest form of it is billboards.

I don't care if they're the old-school kind or those glowing grids of pixels; they need to go. Take all of that garbage down. Restore our sight lines to the Wasatch Mountains. Thousands of square feet of sky reappearing overnight, and no more rectangular shadows. Take them all down, make a stack, and call it Poverty Flats; as in, these things cheapen what it means to be gifted with eyes.

There's no way the hawks will miss them. And somehow we'll still find hamburgers. And if $6,520 per day seems high for a fine, "Too bad," I'll tell our legislature. "Would you rather have miles of nudity? Because my other plan is all billboards have to go nude."

I don't mean photos of naked people; I just mean the word: "Sleep Inn Nudity," "Truck Stop Nudity," "Timpanogos Regional Hospital—Not Bigger. Just Better Nudity," "Cabela's Outdoor Nudity Gear," "Bank of America Nudity Checking," and so on ... "Make America Nude Again."

That should spur the Utah crowds to pull them down if nothing else will. First, an inhale of shock, then some well-deserved destruction. You could hear it from Salt Lake City to Ultimatum Ridge.

METEOROLOGY

There's a writer, Brady Udall, I figure a ton of people already love or at least have heard about. He's good. He's from out West here—northern Arizona, southern Utah—and in his first book, *Letting Loose the Hounds*, there's a story called "Vernon" I won't go into very much except to tell you about one detail: this dead guy's giant woodpile. It's enormous. Almost Cascade-Mountain-sized. Anyway, it's hard to overlook, and yet it disappears into the background of the larger story about three 21-year-old friends.

A story's landscape can do that, fade away a little, since it's the characters' actions or inactions that tend to interest us the most. The thing is, though, this woodpile is more than a part of the setting. Yes, it's a hang-out spot for them, a vantage point from which to see their town, the pine woods, the surrounding mountains, and maybe even the sheriff's wife (we're told she's got quite a body) who is rumored to do her yard work in the nude. And yes, it's there to give the narrator a chance to imagine epic endings—lighting a fire so big you can see it from Mars, or maybe making a misstep so the three of them get avalanched. But it's also a symbol calling out, "Less ant, more grasshopper." Why split and pile up so much wood you can't burn it all in one lifetime? And remember the guy who did this is already dead.

Literature, from *Gather ye rosebuds* to *Waiting for Godot*, is full of this same story. It doesn't wear out. How come? Because we don't listen.

Though that's too simple, of course. Take Sam: He's an honors student, and also has some important job as a liaison on campus. He's wearing a suit and tie and a backpack when I see him. We say, "Hey," and I ask, "How's it going?" and he says, "Fine. Just looking for a hole to crawl into for a couple hours to study." Good for him. What am I doing? I'm walking around, taking a break in the middle of writing this. Good for me. I'm the point guard of the Grasshoppers, at least for now.

And it's not as if I'm un-conflicted about it. I've got drafts of freshman essays all over my desk that aren't going to fix themselves. I got one—one!—done before I moved them aside and started writing this instead.

I also don't own an umbrella. There isn't much point in Utah. I had one once in the old days in Tacoma, but it broke—sideways March winds about 40 miles an hour; 40-degree rain blasts, driven and determined; umbrellas held shoulder high like nylon shields 'til they flipped, inverted, turned inside-out and rib-snapped. I never replaced it. It rained, and I got wet, like this was a deal we'd worked out together, a deal that suited the rain and me just fine ...

I don't know enough about neurons to explain it, but thinking of the rain just now reminds me of The Day of the Quail. They took over the neighborhood. There must have been eighty—I finally stopped counting, that's how many—going by in this surprising line, a group of grown-ups leading the way, then dozens of these jellybean chicks skittering behind. Right down the middle of my street, then left around the corner. I would have liked it even more if there'd been rain to go along with this—*Ah-ha*, that's the connection—but never mind. It was cool.

I told my neighbor Mike about it a couple minutes later, and he took off and started knocking on doors, gathered a group to go catch up and see them. He even stopped traffic on 900 East so all those quail could get safely to the park. He likes birds. And everyone was happy. They were glad that they'd stopped whatever they were doing, glad that they'd slowed down.

You know who wasn't, who didn't want to?—the people in cars.

Or maybe their cars were in charge of the driving, and the cars didn't think there was time to pull over, cut their engines for a while, and have a look.

ZOOLOGY

My neighbor Mike has added an extra ecosystem to his yard. Nothing elaborate, just a daily pile of birdseed next to some groundcover bushes and vines, but it brings all sorts of birds around. Mice too. And other animals up the food chain.

One morning, for instance, when my son Jameson was four, he asked from behind me in his car seat, "What is that?" ... and when I couldn't find it, "In our little tree."

We'd just pulled up to the curb out front—no snow on the ground yet, so this must have been November—and there it was: a hawk, exactly bark colored, improbably big for the branch it was perched on, eight feet away from the sparrow zone, waiting. And we waited too.

Another time it was my cat next door, as tensed and patient as a spring-loaded sphinx, his eyes trained just beyond the birdseed on those vines. He knew there were mice there.

There's another story that's sort of like this and sort of not. It has to do with a sea lion up in Seattle—very smart or very lazy, depending on your attitude; resourceful or greedy, take your pick. He was camping out at the Ballard Locks, right in front of the fish ladder, since to get from Puget Sound back to Lake Washington, and then on again to their spawning rivers, the salmon needed a way to climb around. Park your blubber, open your mouth, and they practically swim right in.

They finally put him on a cargo plane, flew him all the way to Baja, but *damn if that sea lion didn't swim right back.*

I can't help wishing that poetry did that too, incited that same sort of patience and pilgrimage. An open book like a fish ladder. Images like birdseed. People all spring-coiled and waiting, ready for something to step from the greenery: maybe a haiku—

> Hate is a shovel,
> love is a river. Both dig.
> But one just digs holes—

or a sonnet, or even a simple blessing: "May your talons and foreclaws and spirits be sharp. May you find your way back from the Baja coast to eat a hundred poems."

MARINE BIOLOGY

As a kid growing up in Washington, I had a giant admiration for Slick Watts. "Downtown" Freddie Brown too, of course, swishing rainbow jumpers from deep. If they'd had the 3-point line back then, forget about it; you would've needed a pinball machine to keep score.

Slick Watts was first, though. Slick Watts of the Seattle SuperSonics: bald in a league full of afros or longish hair. He wore a headband when nobody else did. He invented the scoop shot! And if I'm misremembering—if others deployed it too—then I don't want to know. Slick Watts ruled, and I used to imitate him while going against invisible defenders in my driveway.

But if you're betting that I liked the Seahawks too, you lose. *Nunca. Nada.* By the time they added Tampa Bay and Seattle, I was already a wild-thing Raiders' fan. I used to run through other kids' arm tackles, thinking (maybe even chanting aloud) "Mark van Eeghen, Mark van Eeghen." I watched Kenny Stabler's 1974 miracle pass to Clarence Davis, knocking the Dolphins from the playoffs; what a happiness launch pad! And I saw Rob Lytle fumble in front of the goal line, saw the Raiders recover, saw the referees conspire to give the Denver Broncos the ball back and a free pass to Super Bowl XII. Which they lost, karmically, 27 to 10.

Anyway, sports. I'm saying I liked them a bit.

So when it came time to write a report on a famous person's biography, who do you think I picked?

Jacques Cousteau. The ocean's own Messenger Angel.

Before him, everyone who wanted to explore underwater had to do it like Captain Nemo, wearing that lead-boots/air-hose contraption dreamt up by—no kidding—Leonardo da Vinci; that's how dated the design was. Well, Jacques Cousteau wanted to swim not trundle, so he went to work inventing scuba gear: self-contained underwater breathing apparatus. The fact that he used English for the acronym is just further proof he knew what he was doing. Americans had all the televisions. It was mainly to kids like me that he was bringing the Good News. I'm saying, when I grew up I wanted to play in the NFL or NBA, but I wanted to *be* Jacques Cousteau.

I planned on majoring in Marine Biology, but it didn't work out that way. Instead, I went with literature and writing, and I can't say I regret it. A lot of the time, though, I find myself writing about sharks; or the coastline, seagulls, coral reefs, humpbacks, manta rays, salmon, and waves. Jungians and astrologers could probably offer reasons, even interesting ones that I might be glad to hear. A mermaid could offer her take on it, saying some are more spell-cast than others. I don't know. Love isn't easy to quantify. It's easier just to praise it, so why not?

STANDING AT HALF MOON BAY STATE BEACH, FACING WEST: A SHARK SONG

I like how they live, the way they hunt sea lions,
the way they attack those meat loaves
when they flop in off the rocks.
What glorious feeding:
the silent, giant hunger underwater
with its blank eyes, gallery of teeth,
its jaws thrown forward, impossibly wide,
then down with dispassion, thrashing
its catch—a bloody avalanche—
ripping out a hundred pounds each bite,
returning through clouds of torn blubber for more,
the dorsal fin cutting like a scythe ...
what glorious food: seals full of salmon
full of grunion spiced with krill.
I remember Thanksgiving at a rich friend's home,
having goose stuffed with duck stuffed with quail,
all seasoned with tangerine blossoms and cloves,
basted in whiskey,
served with a sauce from currants and plums.
It's got to be heaven tearing in.
It must be god-like
to survive a million years, to be perfected:
Devourer of Ocean Life, Terror to Man,
absolutely unmoved by and worthy of our praise ...
may they outlast us.
May the seas swim with good things to eat.

RACCOON VERSES

THERE USED TO BE A TIME WHEN FOXES WERE BROWN

In the Old Songs about Washington, a raccoon and fox
had an argument, each one bragging
that he was the better thief.
The fox stole some colors from the sunset
and painted, for himself, the first flowers,
but the raccoon grabbed their pollen
and gave it to bees to carry everywhere.
The fox got mad.
And more bold.
He picked the lock and entered

the Land of the Dead: endless bones to gnaw on.
Quiet as a current, the raccoon followed.
Quickly, while the fox was eating, he took
and hid the door,
and in the Old Songs, this was good;
it meant the living and dead could now speak.
The fox saw one last chance to even the score:
He poked a paw into Thunder's pocket,
trying to swipe a streak of lightning,
and the flash, if you listen to the Old Songs,
burned his fur the colors of smoke and fire.

That's an origin story about the color of foxes, so the raccoon's just a minor character. He isn't even the antagonist since the fox is really his own worst problem. But the minor character is the one on my mind because the other morning I saw a baby raccoon and was glad that I did.

So were Jen and Quentin and Jameson. And so were our neighbors who kept a kind of casual vigil while he slept all day and evening in their tree.

He'd been moving around under their groundcover vines in this spot where cats like to hide and ambush birds, so I figured he was just a cat until he strolled out onto the grass: this baby raccoon. I got my boys to come and look, but by then he'd gone up the tree, walking up the branches the way that you and I would walk down the sidewalk. And that's where he was, still napping, when my wife Jen got home in the afternoon.

If he were a bird, so what? But he wasn't. He was rare.

And I think that's what a poem is too: this unexpected creature stepping out from under our language and climbing up a tree. And you there to notice.

I like that definition: Poems are raccoons. I like it for two reasons; first, because it's easy to remember, and second because it doesn't make sense unless you're thinking in metaphor and imagery. I'll bet that's how Williams felt after he'd written his famous wheelbarrow poem. I mean, I don't know for sure, but it doesn't seem impossible since a poem is a well-made language contraption, and if you're willing to pay attention, it can take our daily crap-loads and roll them away.

I'm going to try to imitate that same kind of balance now and circle back to foxes and raccoons:

WHY THE RACCOON'S TAIL HAS STRIPES

A fox is a fox—bright
zigzag, cunning stomach—but who is Raccoon,
which way do his whiskers point?
You can knock all day on that question; nobody's home,
just a key beneath the welcome mat,
and inside,
hanging from his ceiling,
strange chandeliers:
arrangements of keys and hoop earrings,
loose change forever going missing,
the silver promises of corkscrews,
laughter, desire...anything shiny.
All those years spent collecting—
here they are.
He isn't a thief; he just looks like a bandit.
Take back whatever you like.
He knows his tail is a lesson in perspective:
Find it/Lose it, Have it/Vanish, making stripes.

COMMONPLACE BEASTS AND WHERE TO FIND THEM

My Front Yard:

I have a squirrel. Not a pet, a visitor. That's important. It makes a difference.

He started coming around last year, with his six movements-and-stillnesses per second, hanging around with the birds at the feeder, his cheeks like pictures of Dizzy Gillespie. And this year he's back.

I wasn't sure he would be because in January I'd seen a dead squirrel in the road—run over on 900 East, a few leaps from Fairmont Park—and worried it was him. But it wasn't. He showed up again in April, zigzagging over to the porch steps, then backflip-sprinting to the tree trunk to execute a perfect leap-cling maneuver. Then he jumped down to break the pogo speed record, then sat in the grass, his tail like a question mark, watching while I went to get the mail. Like I was the interesting one ...

The Floor of My Living Room:

... but I wasn't. I can't move like that. I can barely even describe it.

Especially not now, because my cat keeps using my pen as a chin scratcher, and he's licking my arm to help groom me. He's shedding a Maine coon fur-storm in advance of the coming heat wave, so he probably figures that I should be doing that too. And now his paws and head are on my forearm, which he's holding down and using as a pillow, and my lack of total stillness is earning me a stare. I can see his point—and I'm trying to write without moving—but just like I can't go face first down a tree trunk, I can't use a pen without moving at least a little bit.

Herman Franks Ballpark, Salt Lake City:

A while back the coaches threw an End-of-the-Season Party for the little leaguers: burgers, a few contests, a few raffles, and an Iron Man piñata.

For Jameson, the piñata was the highlight, but it turns out I liked it too because when the bat finally blasted it open and all the eight-year-olds became a scramble-crouch of grabbing, Jameson just tracked the head flying off and picked that up instead: packed full of candy and easy to carry. Pretty smart.

In the ecosystem of childhood, it was like a sudden evolution.

Parkland, Washington:

I saw a squirrel pull a similar trick one summer when I was still a student at PLU (Pacific Lutheran University). This was in front of the library, just off the quad—the grass part with all the cedar trees not the red brick plaza in front of Eastvold Hall.

A girl was sitting on a bench, having lunch (a bag of McDonald's, a strawberry shake) and feeding her fries to a squirrel. She'd toss one. He'd eat it. She'd toss another, and so on, 'til the squirrel was close enough to take them from her hand. She turned away to get another, and that's when the squirrel made off with her shake, clutching and running like a leapfrog, a bounding miracle, straight for a tree, and the girl coming after: *"Hey!"*

The trunk is what stumped him; he wound up dropping the cup while scaling it, which is how I know the shake was strawberry. All this neon pink *splopped* out on the ground.

On the TV News:

Even without the sound on, you can tell the politicos are lying. Impossible to look that smug without lying first to themselves.

Tonight and Tomorrow:

My cat is already sleeping again, and I'd rather be up instead of lying here. But he's 90 now in human years, and limping from what seems like hip pain, and he won't drink water for the last two days, so I'm sticking nearby for quiet company. My smell is a smell he's known forever. And his ears twitch slightly from the sound of pen on paper. And I'm glad my squirrel wasn't the one run over.

But in the morning I hope my cat goes out, and then stalks him from the mailbox to the moon.

TAKE THE A) SEX QUIZ, B) PERSONALITY TEST, OR C) QUICK BREAK FROM BUSYWORK

1. Would you rather be a cheetah or an antelope?
2. Would you rather be an orca or a wolf?
3. If you answered cheetah and orca, go to 4; if cheetah and wolf, proceed to 6. If you answered antelope with either, skip to 23, one for each hour you'll be running. That's the trade-off for looking delicious ... that, and a diet of grasses, maybe iris bulbs if you're fortunate and the rains have

done your digging for you since your ungulate hooves aren't famous for scooping dirt.

4. Congratulations, you're amphibious, fast in both Africa and ocean.
5. But you lack the resonance of wolfsong and whalesong. Someone's got a sexier voice.
6. Congratulations, you're a miracle, capable of hairpin turning at 60 combined with the stamina to hunt for forty miles. You're canine and feline, Northern Hemisphere and Southern, night and day. But also fractured. A wild rift, a howling schism, and
7. perfect as scissors, I agree, but
8. the world isn't paper, it's rock.
9. And you orcas, I haven't forgotten you. I see you raising your dorsal fins. I can hear you thinking *There's nothing wrong with my voice. My squeaks are expressive. I run my meetings efficiently*. Go to ten.
10. Certainty's less creative than doubt. It puts a minute-hand on every circle.
11. Doubt is what rounds some circles into spheres. It's what taught us that we don't fall off.
12. You're darn right that's a paradox.
13. Doubt is that catch, then rising, in the wolf's song. After which longing seems longer ...
14. when will it come, our best moment? When will it come, that feeling we're imagining?
15. Let's turn our attention to fruit now: Would you rather have cherries or watermelon?
16. Good questions. I'll answer them one at a time.
17. Yes, the watermelon's real, not seedless.

18. Yes, the cherries are Rainiers.
19. The watermelon's 19¢-a-lb. You can slice it however you want to.
20. The Rainiers come from a roadside stand. It's hot, but it isn't breezeless.
21. If you answered cherries, go to 25. You get an extra hour for just enjoying.
22. If you answered watermelon, good for you, though any fruit would be perfect...except bananas; that's where we draw the line, and I know a dog who would back me on that—Dennis and Gloria Martin's springer spaniel, Pacific Lutheran University, some dozen or more of us invited over, food laid out on the table, wine and whiskey. And Edith Piaf on the stereo, reinventing singing. And their dog enjoying the party—so many hands, so willingly reaching things for her: grapes and carrots and baba ghanouj, sourdough rolls and smoked salmon, turkey wrapped around Irish cheddar, tartelettes with marzipan, blackberry pie, and all of it good. Except bananas. Bananas were a definite *Nyet*, which reminds me,
23. I didn't pick antelope, you did. You chose *Gravity-defying Rangeland Lightning*. But along with that comes restlessness and troubled sleep.
24. Now think of your favorite sexual position. Go ahead, this quiz can wait for a minute... Is the person you're picturing doing this with more Orca, Wolf, or Cherries; more Gravity-defying or Hairpin-turn; or All-of-the-Above?
25. I think our work here is almost done. A final question ought to wrap it:
26. If you could do one thing a second time, what would it be?

ABOUT ROB CARNEY

Rob Carney grew up in the Pacific Northwest but has lived the last 23 years in Salt Lake City, Utah. He's the author of seven books of poems, most recently *Facts and Figures* (Hoot 'n' Waddle 2020), and *The Book of Sharks* (Black Lawrence Press 2018), which was a finalist for the 2019 Washington State Book Award. In 2014 he received the Robinson Jeffers/Tor House Foundation Award for Poetry. His work has appeared in *Cave Wall*, *The American Journal of Poetry*, and many others, as well as the Norton anthology *Flash Fiction Forward* (2006). He's a Professor of English at Utah Valley University and writes a regular feature called "Old Roads, New Stories" for *Terrain.org*.

ACKNOWLEDGEMENTS AND PERMISSIONS

Thank you to Simmons Buntin, Editor of *Terrain.org*, in which earlier versions of these pieces first appeared:

"Truth > The News" (16 June 2019), "Traveling Through Time" (5 Apr. 2019), "Down Here on the Cold, Cold Ground" (13 Feb. 2019), "I'd Rather Be a Hawk" (1 Oct. 2018), "In the Beginning Was the Word" (17 Aug. 2018), "Environmental Clean-up" (28 May 2018), "Seven Seeds" (1 Apr. 2018), "What Would You Do with a Mini Canoe?" (9 Mar. 2018), "Two Cures for Billboards" (10 Feb. 2018), "Poetry as Collage" (29 Dec. 2017), "Seven Birds" (22 Nov. 2017), "Modern Legacies" (8 Nov. 2017), "Downhill Switchbacks

Ahead" (25 Sept. 2017), "Win $300.00" (24 Aug. 2017), "Raccoon Verses" (2 Aug. 2017), "Commonplace Beasts and Where to Find Them" (14 July 2017), "Wine Is Rain in Translation" (27 May 2017), "Learning from Birds" (10 May 2017), "In the Beginning Was a River" (26 Apr. 2017), "Maybe Not Eden, but Some Kind of Garden" [under the title "History of Drama"] (15 Mar. 2017), "Marine Biology" (4 Jan. 2017), "Architecture" [under the title "Architecture II"] (9 Nov. 2016), "Poetry" (12 Oct. 2016), "Civics Lessons" [under the title "Civics"] (28 Sept. 2016), "Archaeology" (14 Sept. 2016), "Architecture II" [under the title "Architecture"] (24 Aug. 2016), "Environmental Studies" (3 Aug. 2016), "Take the A) Sex Quiz, B) Personality Test, or C) Quick Break from Busywork" [under the title "Sex/Personality"] (20 July 2016), "Political Science" (29 June 2016), "Linguistics" (25 May 2016), "Music History II" (4 May 2016), "Music History" (27 Apr. 2016), "Zoology" (13 Apr. 2016), "Meteorology" (16 Mar. 2016), "Electrical Engineering" (4 Mar. 2016), "Addition + Subtraction" (19 Feb. 2016), "Social Studies" (28 Jan. 2016), "Spelling" (7 Jan. 2016), "Gravitational Pull" (16 Dec. 2015), "How to Carve a Pumpkin" [under the title "Folklore"] (29 Oct. 2015), "Evolution" (14 Oct. 2015), "Trigonometry" (9 Sept. 2015).

"Addition + Subtraction" was accepted for production in an evening of monologues called *The Strand Project 2017*, a theatrical collaboration between Selah Dinner Theater and Lit Youngstown, with performances on June 2nd and 3rd, and June 9th and 10th, 2017, in Struthers, OH.

"Poetry" and "Raccoon Verses" appeared as Parts 1 and 2 of "A Field Guide to Poems in Three Parts" in the book *Far*

Villages: Welcome Essays for New and Beginner Poets, Abayomi Animashaun, editor (New York: Black Lawrence Press, 2019).

"In the Beginning Was a River," "Modern Legacies," and "Music History II" appeared as sections 1, 4, and 6 of "Seven Rivers" in *Tales from the River*, Donna Mulvenna and Margi Prideaux, editors (Parndana: Stormbird Press, 2018).

"Addition + Subtraction" appeared in *Awake in the World: Riverfeet Anthology*, Daniel J. Rice, editor (Bemidji, MN and Livingston, MT: Riverfeet Press, 2017).

"Environmental Studies," "In the Beginning Was a River," and "Seven Seeds" were reprinted by *The Dark Mountain Project* online, Nick Hunt, editor (29 Aug. 2018).

"In the Beginning Was a River" was reprinted online in *About Place Journal: Dignity as an Endangered Species in the 21st Century*, Pam Uschuk, editor (1 May 2019).

"Political Science" was reprinted online by *Escape into Life* (4 July 2018).

DIVE INTO THE STORMBIRD COMMUNITY

where story develops deeper, stronger connections to transform the world.

Stories about our world, and our relationship with nature, have been told by wise souls and changemakers for countless generations. We've gathered around campfires and sat under the limbs of mighty trees to be nurtured by their wisdom. Story is how we've shared moral tales, empowered ourselves with knowledge, and paid hope forward into the future.

Our authors embody the spirit of those changemakers. They write with reverence, wisdom, and inspiration about the places, plants and animals, habitats and ecosystems, of our shared home—*Earth*.

There is no better place to connect with these stories than through the Stormbird Community. We will gift you eBooks and other content that stimulate your mind and heart. In a new philosophical place we call *The Gathering* we'll connect you directly with our brave authors and other bold thinkers. We'll invite you into exciting discussions, but we'll also listen and allow you to explore.

Dive into the current of Stormbird's stories as they soar like feathers in the wind.

SCAN ME

Stormbird Press

www.StormbirdPress.com

CPSIA information can be obtained
at www.ICGtesting.com
Printed in the USA
LVHW090906290321
682812LV00001B/15

9 781925 856293